Eating For Life:

100 Healthful Recipes
from The Kansas City Star

BY JILL WENDHOLT SILVA

Eating for Life:
100 Healthful Recipes from The Kansas City Star
By Jill Wendholt Silva

Published by Kansas City Star Books
1729 Grand Boulevard
Kansas City, Missouri USA 64108

© Copyright 2007 The Kansas City Star Co.

Written and edited by Jill Wendholt Silva
Design by Amy Robertson
Photography by Jim Barcus, David Eulitt, Tammy Ljungblad,
Rich Sugg and Jill Toyoshiba.

First edition

ISBN: 978-1-933466-47-7

Printed by Walsworth Publishing Co., Marceline, Mo.

To order copies, call StarInfo at 816-234-4636 (say "operator").
To order online, go to www.TheKansasCityStore.com.

**KANSAS CITY STAR
BOOKS**

Contents

Foreword

Carbs are good. Carbs are bad. Drink juice. Don't drink juice. Use margarine instead of butter. Use butter instead of margarine. Eat this. Don't eat that.

Americans spend billions of dollars each year on various weight-loss products, yet we continue to eat too much and move too little, which is leading to an epidemic of overweight adults and children in our country.

But with all the conflicting nutrition and diet information out there it can be extremely difficult to decipher what is true science and what is the latest diet fad misinformation. As a nutrition spokesperson and registered dietitian for the Kansas City Chiefs and Kansas City Royals, I know it can be difficult to put complicated scientific information into realistic, convenient and quick strategies that work well for my busy clients. And whether you are a professional athlete, corporate executive, or stay-at-home mom, your nutrition goals are often quite similar: to lose weight and maximize energy levels.

In 1995, I moved to San Francisco to complete my clinical nutrition training at the University of California, San Francisco. After living in a culinary mecca, I wasn't so sure what to expect when I returned home in 2001.

One of the things that impressed me most was The Kansas City Star food section. A dietitian's delight, I was thrilled to see not only the great food information but also an emphasis on nutrition! Wow, I had not seen that before!

I was so intrigued by the quality of information I contacted the food editor. Over coffee, Jill Silva eagerly shared the evolution of The Star's weekly Eating for Life column. I learned about her commitment and passion to share accurate and practical nutrition information to readers.

We share many of the same philosophies about food and nutrition: first and foremost, we both love food! And we both know that weight control revolves around a balanced diet, plus exercise.

The Kansas City community is fortunate to have someone who is so dedicated to communicating sound nutrition information on the pages of our hometown newspaper. Eating For Life: 100 Healthful Recipes From The Kansas City Star features delicious, easy-to-fix recipes with gorgeous color photos of each dish.

Eating for Life should be your go-to cookbook for easy, nutritious and delicious meals and fact-based nutrition information. I feel very fortunate to have such a high-quality cookbook to recommend to my clients so whether you want to lose weight, improve energy, or just eat more nutritiously, Eating for Life can help you reach your goals!

— Mitzi Dulan, RD
Sports Nutritionist,
Kansas City Chiefs and Kansas City Royals
www.nutritionexpert.com.

Author's Introduction

The *Star's* weekly "Eating for Life" column grew out of two award-winning series: Nutrition for Life (May 2003) and Eating for Life (March 2004).

Initially I was reluctant to tackle nutrition topics, a beat with science that is often confusing and conflicting. The accuracy and attention to detail required for nutrition reporting seemed beyond the scope of a daily newspaper section with a staff of one.

But my assistant managing editor, Mary Lou Nolan, was eager to provide readers with more health and nutrition coverage, and when the first series appeared, I think everyone was surprised by the reader response.

While Nutrition for Life focused on the social and cultural changes that had led America to the brink of an obesity crisis, Eating for Life focused on the ways average home cooks could tweak their diets to improve their health. We featured 27 original recipes developed by Kansas City-based home economists Kathryn Moore and Roxanne Wyss.

The goal was to create recipes that follow the USDA's Dietary Guidelines. The focus is on the fundamentals of a balanced diet: lean cuts of meat, low-sodium products, whole grains, fresh fruits and vegetables and reduced serving sizes. Each recipe includes nutritional analysis.

The response to Eating for Life was so positive it grew into a weekly column. The "Eating for Life" column debuted in May 2005 and continues to appear on the McClatchy-Tribune News Services where it was picked up by member newspapers as far away as Anchorage, Alaska.

We hope you enjoy these simple, healthful family-style recipes. For more, check out *The Star's* Food section each week or go to KansasCity.com.

— *Jill Wendholt Silva, Food Editor*

Biographies

Jill Wendholt Silva has been *The Star's* food editor since 1993. She has won numerous awards for her food journalism, including the James Beard Award for Best Section and writing awards from the Association of Food Journalists. She has been writing the weekly "Eating for Life" column which has appeared in The Star's Food section since May 2005. The weekly column has been honored by the Kansas City chapter of The Society of Professional Journalists and is distributed by McClatchy-Tribune News Services appearing in member newspapers across the country.

Kathryn Moore and Roxanne Wyss are Kansas City-based food consultants and home economists. They consult with many food and appliance companies, writing recipes, testing products, developing instructions and setting the standard for clear, concise, yet innovative recipes and food information. Their original recipes have been featured in many advertisements and on package labels. They also appear regularly on television and radio shows in cities throughout the country.

Betsy Mann provides recipe analysis for several major metropolitan newspapers, including The Star. All recipes were analyzed by the MasterCook Deluxe computer software program.

Staff photographer **David Eulitt** worked on the initial Eating for Life series. Staff photographer **Tammy Ljungblad** has produced the bulk of photography for the Eating for Life columns, with additional work by staff photographers **Jim Barcus**, **Jill Toyoshiba** and **Rich Sugg**.

All food was styled by **Jill Wendholt Silva**.

The Eating for Life cookbook was designed by **Amy Robertson**.

Special thanks to *Star* editors **Mary Lou Nolan, Cindy Hoedel, Joe Ledford** and **Mary Schulte** for their support.

Special thanks to **Norma Martin** for her vision and encouragement in getting the column off the ground.

As always, I am indebted to my family, **Otavio, André** and **Daniela**. — J.W.S.

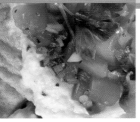

Appetizers, Salads And Soups

Photo by Tammy Ljungblad • THE KANSAS CITY STAR

Dive Into This Dip

Dips are rarely skinny, so chances are you've sworn off the high-calorie party food at one time or another.

But you don't have to banish dips altogether. Sure, typical dairy-based dips tend to be high in saturated fat, but choosing lower-fat dairy products can let the good times roll.

The Star's festive Tomato Basil Cheese Spread starts with a base of low-fat ricotta cheese. Smoother than cottage cheese, ricotta is made by "recooking" the whey, which is the watery liquid that separates from the curds in cheese-making.

Traditionally used to make lasagna, ravioli or manicotti, ricotta has been slimming down in recent years.

A 1-ounce serving of fat-free ricotta has 27 calories, 5 grams of protein, 1 gram carbohydrates and 27 milligrams of sodium, according to drgourmet.com, a Web site featuring Timothy Harlan, an internist and a chef.

Readily available in the dairy case of supermarkets, ricotta is also a rich source of dietary calcium. It also is high in protein, phosphorous and selenium.

When combined with goat cheese, the mild-tasting ricotta takes on a delicious tang.

Doubling up again, the cheeses are garnished with two types of tomato. Fresh tomatoes provide lycopene, an antioxidant that may prevent prostate cancer, heart disease and skin ailments, but intensely flavored bits of sun-dried tomato concentrate the benefits of lycopene. Even better, lycopene is more available to the body when served in combination with a tablespoon of olive oil.

Fresh basil and toasted pine nuts add interest and a fresh Italian flavor, so go ahead and dig in. Just don't double dip.

Tomato Basil Cheese Spread

Makes 8 to 10 appetizer servings

1 cup low-fat ricotta cheese
3 ounces fresh goat cheese
1/3 cup sun-dried tomatoes, dry packed
2 cloves garlic, minced
2 to 3 Roma tomatoes, seeded and diced
1/4 cup chopped fresh basil leaves
1 tablespoon extra-virgin olive oil
1/4 teaspoon salt
1/4 teaspoon freshly ground pepper
1 tablespoon pine nuts, toasted
Basil leaves for garnish, optional
30 reduced fat whole-wheat crackers

Shopping Tip:
For a taste
twist, try smoke-
flavored sun-dried
tomatoes.

Place ricotta and goat cheese in bowl; beat with a mixer until smooth. Spread cheese mixture evenly in a small shallow dish; cover and refrigerate.

Using kitchen shears, cut dried tomato into small pieces. Cover with boiling water and allow to stand 20 to 30 minutes or until softened. Drain well on paper towels.

Combine sun-dried tomatoes, garlic, Roma tomatoes, basil, olive oil, salt and pepper. Toss gently to blend, then spoon evenly over cheese. Sprinkle with pine nuts. Garnish with fresh basil. Serve with crackers.

Per serving, based on 8: 193 calories (41 percent from fat), 9 grams total fat (4 grams saturated), 24 milligrams cholesterol, 17 grams carbohydrates, 11 grams protein, 602 milligrams sodium, 2 grams dietary fiber.

SERVING TIP: Instead of chips, serve with a whole-wheat cracker.

The Life Of The Party

Photo by Jim Barcus • THE KANSAS CITY STAR

Bet you've heard this one before: Noshing on high-fat, high-salt appetizers at parties can be a diet disaster.

Enough spinach-artichoke dip, already!

Admittedly, it's not easy to come up with healthy yet festive party snacks. But we pondered until we came up with an appetizer that could provide the proper panache for any fete.

And the ah-ha ingredient?

Horseradish.

Any time you're looking for a low-fat condiment to add zing, horseradish packs a flavor punch. The Star's Marinated Party Shrimp appetizer features a zingy sauce featuring horseradish, chili sauce, hot pepper sauce and capers. Pour it over the shrimp and allow them to marinate for a few hours in the refrigerator.

Once thought to be a food to avoid because it is high in cholesterol, shrimp is—again—the life of the party. It turns out the cholesterol in shrimp does not elevate blood cholesterol levels. Plus, shrimp is low in saturated fat, the real culprit for elevated cholesterol levels in most people.

A rich source of protein, shellfish is a good source of iron, B12, omega-3 fatty acids, selenium and zinc. These nutrients protect against anemia, arthritis, cancer, cardiovascular disease, cataracts, depression and infertility.

PUMP IT UP: For a festive presentation, place several shrimp in martini glasses and serve an elegant shrimp cocktail to partygoers.

Marinated Horseradish Party Shrimp

Makes 12 to 14 appetizer servings

1/4 cup chili sauce
1 tablespoon prepared horseradish
2 tablespoons lemon juice
2 tablespoons Dijon mustard
1 tablespoon extra-virgin olive oil
1 teaspoon hot pepper sauce
3 cloves garlic, minced
2 green onions, sliced
2 tablespoons capers, rinsed and drained
2 pounds peeled large shrimp, cooked
Green leaf lettuce, cut into thin shreds

Mix together chili sauce, horseradish, lemon juice, mustard, olive oil, hot sauce and garlic. Add onions and capers. Pour over shrimp and toss lightly to coat well. Cover and refrigerate 1 to 2 hours before serving. Place lettuce on serving platter and top with shrimp.

Per serving, based on 12: 96 calories (25 percent from fat), 3 grams total fat (trace saturated fat), 115 milligrams cholesterol, 2 grams carbohydrates, 16 grams protein, 164 milligrams sodium, trace dietary fiber.

COOKING TIP: If you don't want to dirty any dishes, simply pour the sauce into a zip-top plastic food bag, add shrimp, close bag and gently work mixture around until shrimp is thoroughly coated. Pour shrimp on serving platter and discard the bag.

Shopping Tip: Choose "large" shrimp for this recipe, which is 21 to 30 shrimp per pound. If you want to save time, ask the seafood department at your supermarket to steam the shrimp.

Trick Your Taste Buds

Photo by Tammy Ljungblad • THE KANSAS CITY STAR

Sight gags are jokes that rely on visual cues rather than words.

Imagine an apricot half positioned over a puddle of plain yogurt to mimic a "fried egg." Or "sushi" made out of Rice Krispies and gummy worms, with fruit leather as a stand-in for the nori wrapper.

Food that appears to be something else is a fun way to get kids to try something new. And the ruse can work on adults, too. The Star's Sweet And Sour Crostini deceives the eyes while it teases the taste buds. In this case, the chopped "olives" are really—gotcha!—raisins.

Why pull the ol' switchroo? Olives are admittedly delicious, but they are high in sodium, so raisins are a smart choice for anyone with high blood pressure. A naturally sweet source of energy, raisins are also rich in iron and potassium. They're high in antioxidants, and studies show they promote oral health.

The red peppers used in the bread topping are extremely high in vitamin C: 1 cup provides more vitamin C (232 milligrams) than the same amount of orange juice (82 milligrams), according to the USDA's nutrient data base at nal.usda.gov/fnic/foodcomp/search. Red peppers also are loaded with phytonutrients such as beta-carotene, which is believed to prevent certain cancers and diseases of the eye and heart.

Finally, we chose a whole-grain rustic bread instead of white bread, which ups the nutrition and fiber content of the crostini, an Italian word that means "little toasts."

Sweet And Sour Crostini

Makes 6 to 8 servings

2 tablespoons dark raisins
1 (7-ounce) jar roasted red peppers,
    well drained and coarsely chopped
3 tablespoons olive oil
2 tablespoons balsamic vinegar
1 small clove garlic, minced
Pinch of salt
Freshly ground pepper to taste
6 slices rustic country bread,
    sliced 1/2-inch thick

Cooking Tip: The pepper mixture can be made up to a day ahead and refrigerated. Just be sure to bring to room temperature before serving.

Place raisins in warm water and allow to plump 5 minutes; drain well. Finely chop raisins.

Combine raisins with peppers, olive oil, vinegar, garlic, salt and pepper; set aside. Toast bread. Cut bread slices in half and top with pepper mixture. Serve immediately.

Per serving, based on 6: 157 calories (44 percent from fat), 8 grams total fat (1 gram saturated), trace cholesterol, 19 grams carbohydrates, 3 grams protein, 180 milligrams sodium, 4 grams dietary fiber.

SHOPPING TIPS: Roasting red peppers in the oven or over a gas flame can be tedious. Instead, look for jarred roasted red peppers in the produce section. Buy an extra jar of red peppers and a stash of raisins to keep in the pantry and you'll always have something on hand to serve when unexpected guests stop by.

Asparagus: Stalks Of Greatness

Photo by Tammy Ljungblad • THE KANSAS CITY STAR

When the Roman emperor Augustus Caesar wanted a quick end to a distasteful task, he'd proclaim: *"Velocius quam asparagi conquantur."*

"Let it be done quicker than you would cook asparagus."

That was, of course, long before the invention of the microwave. These days there's nothing drawn out about steaming the nutritious spring stalks. Luckily the quick-cooking method also naturally preserves precious nutrients.

Since ancient times the luscious grass-green spears have been considered good for what ails you: a remedy for heart trouble and toothaches, an antidote for bee stings, a reproductive tonic and a natural diuretic.

Asparagus has fewer than 25 calories per stalk and is high in folic acid, which may prevent birth defects. The National Cancer Institute has named asparagus the food highest in glutathione, an antioxidant and potent cancer fighter; it also a good source of vitamin A, B6 and C, calcium, iron, thiamin, potassium and fiber.

Too often served drenched in butter or hollandaise sauce, mild, earthy asparagus is just as suited to lighter preparations. *The Star's* Asian Marinated Asparagus bathes the spears in a mixture of low-sodium soy sauce, rice wine vinegar, ginger and lemon. The dish is served cold, and etiquette experts say it's OK to eat the slender stalks with your fingers.

Asian Marinated Asparagus

Makes 4 servings

1 pound asparagus spears
2 tablespoons water
1/4 cup seasoned rice vinegar
2 tablespoons reduced-sodium soy sauce
2 teaspoons chopped fresh ginger
1 teaspoon dark sesame oil
2 teaspoons freshly squeezed lemon juice
Zest of 1 lemon, divided

Remove tough ends and scales from asparagus. Place the stalks in glass pie plate and add water. Cover with a paper towel and microwave on high (100 percent) power 3 minutes or until just tender. Plunge asparagus into cold water and drain well.

Place remaining ingredients in zip-top plastic food bag, reserving 1 teaspoon lemon zest for garnish. Seal, then massage bag to blend well. Add asparagus and reseal bag. Refrigerate overnight or at least 2 hours. Drain marinade and discard. Serve cold.

Per serving: 37 calories (29 percent from fat), 1 gram total fat (trace saturated fat), no cholesterol, 5 grams carbohydrates, 2 grams protein, 302 milligrams sodium, 1 gram dietary fiber.

PREPARATION TIPS: Asparagus grows in sandy soil, so wash tips well to remove any grit. Fresh asparagus is best served the same day it is purchased, but if that is not possible, put stems upright in a container with water as you would a flower bouquet. Cover loosely with a plastic bag and keep in the refrigerator no more than three days.

The natural sugars in asparagus quickly turn to starch. To remove the tough, woody ends, simply hold each stalk, one at a time, between your hands and bend where it naturally breaks.

Shopping Tips: Most of the phytonutrients are in the tips, so choose asparagus with tightly closed tips.

Look for sesame oil in the ethnic foods aisle.

Munch On Powerful Protein

Photo by Tammy Ljungblad • THE KANSAS CITY STAR

Invited to a party?

Offer to bring the appetizers.

Indeed, there's little doubt that the preamble to any meal can torpedo the best of dietary intentions. "Just a few bites," you resolve as you scoop up another chipful of that sinfully creamy dip.

But by the time dinner arrives, you're full. Not to mention you've just downed plenty of added fat and salt.

Choosing those little nibbles wisely before a meal can keep you from making costly missteps—you know, the ones that linger on the hips. The Star's Pico de Gallo Pitas can keep you on the right track. Spread whole-wheat pita triangles with a tangy mashed chickpea dip topped with fresh salsa, and you have a Mediterranean/Mexican fusion twist that's fresh and delicious.

Study the USDA MyPyramid and you'll see beans are an interesting fit. You might think they would be listed under the grains category but the dietary icon groups meat and beans together instead.

That's because beans are an excellent source of protein. A quarter cup of legumes (seeds that grow in pods) is equivalent to 1 ounce of meat, poultry or fish.

Chickpeas, which are alternatively known as garbanzo beans or *ceci*, contain plenty of fiber, folate, iron, magnesium, phosphorous and potassium.

MyPyramid also spotlights the imbalance of sodium and potassium in the typical American diet. Too much salt can lead to hypertension, kidney stones, stroke and heart disease. A potassium-rich diet of leafy green vegetables and legumes can blunt the effects of too much salt.

More than most foods, a serving of beans can also act as a powerful tool in weight control.

The high fiber content makes beans more filling than most other foods. In the stomach, they digest at a slower rate, causing a more gradual rise in blood sugar that, ultimately, keeps hunger at bay longer.

OK, so you might still wind up too full for the burger off the grill, but at least you've made a wise snacking choice in the interim.

Pico de Gallo Pitas

Makes 16 appetizer servings

1/2 cup chopped red pepper
1/2 cup chopped green pepper
2 Roma tomatoes, seeded and chopped
2 tablespoons minced red onion
4 cloves garlic, minced, divided
2 tablespoons minced fresh cilantro
1 tablespoon minced fresh oregano
1 tablespoon freshly squeezed lime juice
Dash of hot pepper sauce
Salt and pepper to taste
1 (15-ounce) can garbanzo beans,
    rinsed and drained
2 tablespoons lemon juice
2 tablespoons water
1/4 cup reduced-fat sour cream
4 whole-wheat flat breads

Cooking Tip: The bean spread can be made in advance and stored in the refrigerator for up to a week.

Preheat oven to 350 degrees. Combine red pepper, green pepper, tomatoes, red onion, 1 clove minced garlic, cilantro, oregano, lime juice and hot pepper sauce. Stir well, then season lightly with salt and pepper. Set aside.

Place garbanzo beans, remaining garlic, lemon juice and water in blender; process until smooth, scraping sides as necessary. Add sour cream and process until combined.

Cut flatbreads into quarters and arrange on baking sheet. Spray with nonstick vegetable cooking spray. Bake 5 to 7 minutes or until hot and crisp. Spread each with about 1 tablespoon bean spread and top with about 1 1/2 tablespoons pico de gallo.

Per serving: 86 calories (8 percent from fat), 1 gram total fat (trace saturated), 1 miligram cholesterol, 17 grams carbohydrates, 3 grams protein, 167 milligrams sodium, 2 grams dietary fiber.

SHOPPING TIP: Although convenient hummus dips are available at most supermarkets, making your own is a snap and can help reduce the amount of sodium. More than 75 percent of salt in the American diet comes from consuming processed foods. To save time, we've gone with canned beans instead. Be sure to rinse to remove most of the sodium added when the beans are processed.

Wrap And Roll

Tired of bread?

Tortillas have been around for ages, but using them as sandwich wraps is an idea that emerged on the food scene more than a decade ago.

Although fast-food restaurants like Chipotle Mexican Grill typically opt for extra-large tortillas, there are other options. *The Star's* Lavosh Wrap features Armenian flatbread made with water, flour, yeast and salt.

Popular throughout the eastern Mediterranean, Iran and the Caucasus, lavosh has two forms. In its hard form, the brittle bread can be kept in the pantry for long periods, much like a cracker. In its soft form, water makes it pliable and easy to wrap any sandwich ingredient.

These appetizers are quick to make, easy to take and allow even non-cooks to look like a party pro.

COOKING TIP: To make lavosh pliable, rinse under cold water and place on the kitchen counter between two slightly damp but clean dish towels. Thirty to 45 minutes later, you have a pliable bread to roll up into a sandwich.

Like learning to wrap a burrito or an egg roll, working with lavosh can have a bit of a learning curve. If you roll the sandwich and it begins to crack or split, use a spray bottle with water to moisten the cracker.

If the lavosh seems too wet, simply allow it to dry out slightly between the towels.

Lavosh Wrap

Makes 8 to 12 appetizer servings

4 (5-inch) large round lavosh
4 tablespoons light garden vegetable cream cheese
1 cup fresh spinach or dark green leafy lettuce
1 large tomato, thinly sliced
7 ounces deli sliced roast beef or lean turkey

Rinse each lavosh round under cold running water for several seconds. Place between muslin or terry towels for 30 to 45 minutes, or until pliable. Spread 1 tablespoon cream cheese on each lavosh. Divide spinach, tomato and deli meat between the 4 lavosh. Roll each lavosh tightly into a wrap-type sandwich. Wrap tightly in plastic wrap.

Refrigerate the sandwich until ready to eat. Cut into pieces with a sharp knife.

Per serving (8): 134 calories (29 percent from fat), 4 grams total fat (1 gram saturated), 14 milligrams cholesterol, 13 grams carbohydrates, 10 grams protein, 461 milligrams sodium, 1 gram dietary fiber.

SHOPPING TIP: Lavosh comes in several sizes. *The Star's* recipe developers used 5-inch rounds; I was able to find a 14-inch pizza-size lavosh. If your supermarket doesn't stock lavosh, look for it at Middle Eastern markets.

If you simply can't find lavosh, feel free to substitute flour tortillas or the Indian flatbread *naan*.

Shopping Tip: Unlike regular sandwich bread, lavosh has a shelf-life of about a year. If you're frequently running out of bread, keeping a couple of lavosh on hand is a good way to avoid a late-night run to the supermarket.

A Hands-On Dish: Lettuce Wraps

Photo by Tammy Ljungblad • THE KANSAS CITY STAR

Google "lettuce wraps" and you'll trip over scores of copycat recipes for P.F. Chang's Chicken Lettuce Wrap. "Just like the real thing!" Heidi75 gushes over the knockoff posted on recipezaar.com.

Once found mostly in Asian restaurants, the lettuce wrap began turning up in mainstream restaurants like the Cheesecake Factory and Chili's a few years ago, and it wasn't long before home cooks were eager to integrate the fun food into their own menus.

Whether you're eating in or out, *The Star's* Chicken Lettuce Wraps are a smart nutrition choice. Bite-size cubes of lean meat are stir-fried in a flavorful sauce and wrapped in a cool, crisp and crunchy vegetable shell.

Dieters have long known that celery and water chestnuts not only enhance the texture of a stir-fry but also are low in calories and sodium and contain no fat or cholesterol.

Meanwhile, mushrooms contain potassium, folate, niacin and copper, which helps the body produce red blood cells and regulate other chemical reactions that are a part of good health.

Studies by the USDA's Agricultural Research Service show that even when stir-fried, mushrooms retain most of their nutrients.

SERVING TIPS: Choose large, pliable lettuce leaves and remove the core if tough. Before serving, separate lettuce and wash in cold water. Drain, place each leaf between paper towels and refrigerate 1 to 2 hours or until crisp.

Chicken Lettuce Wraps

Makes 6 to 8 appetizer servings

Cooking sauce:
1 tablespoon hoisin sauce
2 tablespoons reduced-sodium soy sauce
3 tablespoons water
1 tablespoon dry sherry
2 teaspoons cornstarch
1 teaspoon sesame oil
1/4 teaspoon red pepper flakes

Chicken and vegetables:
1 pound boneless, skinless chicken breasts, cut into 1/4-inch cubes
2 teaspoons dry sherry
1 teaspoon reduced-sodium soy sauce
1 teaspoon cornstarch
1/8 teaspoon pepper
2 tablespoons vegetable oil, divided
1 (8-ounce) can sliced water chestnuts, drained and chopped
2 stalks celery, chopped
1 cup chopped mushrooms
1 teaspoon grated fresh ginger
2 cloves garlic, minced
1 green onion, chopped
6 to 8 large leaves Boston, leaf or iceberg lettuce

Cooking Tip: Reduce red pepper flakes to 1/8 teaspoon if a milder dish is preferred.

For cooking sauce: Blend together hoisin sauce, soy sauce, water, sherry, cornstarch, sesame oil and red pepper flakes. Set aside.

For chicken and vegetables: Combine chicken, sherry, soy sauce, cornstarch and pepper in a bowl; set aside. Be sure the rest of the ingredients are chopped and measured. Heat 1 tablespoon oil in large, nonstick skillet over medium-high heat. Add chicken and cook, stirring frequently, until fully cooked. Remove chicken from skillet, drain and set aside.

Add remaining 1 tablespoon oil to skillet and add chopped water chestnuts, celery and mushrooms. Cook, stirring frequently, 2 minutes. Return chicken to skillet. Stir in ginger and garlic. Stir Cooking Sauce again, then pour over chicken and vegetables. Cook, stirring constantly, 1 to 2 minutes or until sauce is thickened and chicken and vegetables are evenly coated. Remove from heat. Stir in green onion. Divide mixture among lettuce leaves and roll each like a burrito.

Per serving, based on 6: 176 calories (34 percent from fat), 6 grams total fat (1 gram saturated), 44 milligrams cholesterol, 9 grams carbohydrates, 19 grams protein, 344 milligrams sodium, 2 grams dietary fiber.

A Slimming Salad Reduction

Photo by Tammy Ljungblad • THE KANSAS CITY STAR

Chefs have a technique in their culinary arsenal that home cooks should steal: It's called a reduction—and it has absolutely nothing to do with liposuction.

A culinary reduction is made when a chef slowly simmers a liquid, allowing the total volume to reduce to its essence through evaporation. The cider in *The Star's* Romaine And Spinach Salad With Cider House Dressing is eventually reduced to the consistency of syrup. The process concentrates the earthy, naturally spicy flavor of this popular early American beverage.

Although gourmet stores have been peddling exotic flavored vinaigrettes spiked with fruit flavors for years, it's easy and much less expensive to make your own. Plus, this cider reduction cuts the amount of oil down to a mere teaspoon and adds few calories to the dressing.

Pretty to look at, this hearty seasonal salad features a base of good-for-you green lettuce and spinach artfully garnished with the rich, robust flavors of fall: apples, walnuts and dried cranberries.

Each of the salad ingredients adds a layer of good nutrition. For instance, a combination of green and red apples is low in calories, high in flavor and adds a good amount of vitamin C to the diet. Leaving the skin on is not only attractive; it adds fiber.

Walnuts are considered healthful, thanks to their omega-3, a "good" fat that can help reduce the risk of heart disease and lower blood cholesterol.

Dried cranberries add tart sweetness while contributing more vitamin C.

Romaine And Spinach Salad With Cider House Vinaigrette

Makes 6 servings

1 cup apple cider
1/3 cup walnut pieces
2 teaspoons sugar
5 cups torn romaine
4 cups torn spinach
1 small Granny Smith apple, cored and sliced
1 small Red Delicious apple, cored and sliced
2 tablespoons lemon juice
1/2 cup sweetened dried cranberries
2 tablespoons white wine vinegar
1 teaspoon olive oil
1/8 teaspoon salt

Boil apple cider, uncovered, in a small saucepan over medium-high heat, 13 to 14 minutes or until cider is reduced to 3 to 4 tablespoons. Remove from heat and allow to cool completely.

Combine walnuts and sugar in a small skillet. Heat over medium-low heat, stirring constantly, until sugar melts and coats walnuts. Remove from heat and cool completely.

Combine romaine and spinach in large salad bowl. Toss apple slices in lemon juice; drain and add to greens. Sprinkle with cranberries.

Whisk together cooled apple cider syrup, vinegar, olive oil and salt; drizzle over salad and toss to coat. Sprinkle with walnuts.

Per serving: 111 calories (37 percent from fat), 5 grams total fat (trace saturated fat), no cholesterol, 16 grams carbohydrates, 3 grams protein, 66 milligrams sodium, 3 grams dietary fiber.

PREPARATION TIP: Lemon juice helps keep the apple slices from turning brown.

Pump It Up: Spritzing a little extra lemon juice on the salad makes the iron in the spinach more available for your body to use.

A Base For Savory Toppings

Polenta is a popular staple in northern Italy. Similar to Southern-style grits, polenta is cornmeal that can be cooked and eaten as porridge for breakfast or cooled until firm, sliced into wedges and topped with savory toppings for lunch or dinner.

The Star's recipe for Polenta With Italian Vegetables can be served as a vegetarian main course, a side dish or a starter. Made from pantry and freezer staples, the chunky vegetable topping is an easy, economical way to up your vegetable servings.

The mixture includes artichoke hearts, which contain folate, a B vitamin that prevents birth defects, as well as cholesterol-lowering luteolin and cynarin to prevent fat accumulation in the liver. We chose frozen artichokes over canned because they have less sodium.

The mix also includes mushrooms (riboflavin, niacin and vitamin B6), broccoli (beta carotene, calcium, folate and lutein), red peppers (beta carotene, vitamin C and lutein) and tomatoes (beta carotene, vitamin C, lutein and lycopene).

PREPARATION TIPS: Depending on the coarseness of the cornmeal, you may need to adjust the cooking time listed in the recipe. Cook the cornmeal until thick like oatmeal. The spoon should leave a visible mark as you stir.

Photo by Tammy Ljungblad • THE KANSAS CITY STAR

Polenta With Italian Vegetables

Makes 6 servings

Polenta:
3 1/2 cups water
1/2 teaspoon salt
1 cup stone-ground cornmeal
Freshly ground pepper to taste
4 tablespoons grated Parmesan cheese,
    divided

Italian vegetables:
1 tablespoon olive oil
1 medium sweet onion, chopped
3 cloves garlic, minced
1 cup sliced mushrooms
1 cup frozen chopped artichoke hearts, thawed and drained
1 cup frozen chopped broccoli, thawed and drained
2/3 cup chopped roasted red pepper, drained
2 Roma tomatoes, peeled, seeded and chopped
2 1/2 teaspoons Italian seasoning
Salt and pepper to taste
1 (14.5-ounce) can whole no-salt-added tomatoes
2 tablespoons minced fresh parsley

Shopping Tip: Look for 100 percent stone ground whole grain cornmeal, medium grind.

For the polenta: Heat water to a boil in a saucepan. Reduce heat to medium and add salt. Slowly stir in cornmeal and whisk constantly 5 minutes. Continue cooking, stirring with a wooden spoon, 25 minutes. (When done, polenta will almost begin to hold its shape.) Remove from heat. Stir in pepper and 3 tablespoons Parmesan.

Spray a 9-inch springform pan with nonstick vegetable cooking spray. Spoon polenta into pan and smooth. Set aside; cool 30 to 45 minutes. Preheat oven to 375 degrees. Sprinkle top of polenta with remaining Parmesan. Bake 15 to 20 minutes or until lightly set. Allow to stand 5 minutes. Remove sides of pan, cut into 6 wedges and transfer to serving plate.

For the vegetables: Heat olive oil in Dutch oven over medium heat. Add onion and garlic and sauté, stirring frequently, 3 to 4 minutes. Stir in mushrooms and sauté 2 minutes. Stir in remaining ingredients, except parsley and Parmesan. Season with salt and pepper, stirring to break tomatoes into small pieces. Cover, reduce heat and simmer 10 minutes or until tender. Stir in parsley. Spoon vegetables over polenta.

Per serving: 192 calories (20 percent from fat), 4 grams total fat (1 gram saturated), 3 milligrams cholesterol, 33 grams carbohydrates, 7 grams protein, 299 milligrams sodium, 7 grams dietary fiber.

Photo by Tammy Ljungblad • THE KANSAS CITY STAR

When Fennel Is Fantastic

Love it. Hate it. Fennel seems to have that effect on people.

In the supermarket the creamy, bulb-shaped vegetable with feathery green fronds sticking out of it like Martian antennae is often mislabeled as "sweet anise." The comparison can lead anyone who has ever drunk too much ouzo, the licorice-flavored liqueur, to just say no.

Luckily, when used raw, the flavor of fennel is milder and sweeter. It's even less potent when roasted or braised. The Star's recipe for Roasted Fennel And Red Pepper Salad makes a beautiful and healthful salad with a clean, fresh taste.

Fennel is rich in vitamin A and offers fair amounts of calcium, phosphorous and potassium. Red peppers contain loads of beta-carotene, fiber and vitamin B6. Add mixed salad greens and drizzle with olive oil, a heart-healthy monounsaturated fat high in phytonutrients and vitamin E, and you have an impressive start to any meal.

COOKING TIPS: If fennel is new to you, *365 Quick Tips* by the editors of *Cook's Illustrated* magazine gives the lowdown on how to trim the bulb.

Step 1. Cut off stems and feathery fronds. (The fronds can be minced and used as a garnish.)

Step 2. Trim a thin slice from the base of the bulb and remove any tough or blemished outer layers of the bulb.

Step 3. Cut the bulb in half through the base and use a paring knife to cut out the pyramid-shaped piece of the core in each half. The fennel bulb can now be quartered for use in this recipe.

Roasted Fennel
And Red Pepper Salad

Makes 6 servings

1 1/2 to 2 pounds fennel bulbs (about 3 or 4 bulbs)
   trimmed and quartered
2 large red peppers
10 whole mushrooms
2 tablespoons olive oil
3 tablespoons Italian parsley, coarsely chopped
1/4 cup freshly squeezed lemon juice
   (about 1 large lemon)
2 tablespoons sherry vinegar
1 clove garlic, minced
1/3 cup extra-virgin olive oil
Salt and freshly ground pepper to taste
2 to 3 cups spring mix greens
2 tablespoons thinly shaved or grated
   Parmesan cheese, optional

Place fennel in large zip-top plastic food bag. Seed peppers and cut each pepper into fourths; place in bag with fennel. Add mushrooms to bag; drizzle with 2 tablespoons olive oil. Massage vegetables to evenly distribute olive oil. Pour vegetables on large baking sheet and roast at 425 degrees 25 to 30 minutes. Allow to cool slightly, then slice fennel and peppers into thin strips. Quarter mushrooms. Place cut roasted vegetables into mixing bowl. Sprinkle with Italian parsley.

Combine lemon juice, vinegar, garlic and 1/3 cup extra-virgin olive oil. Blend well with small whisk; add salt and pepper.

Drizzle dressing over roasted vegetables and toss to coat. Place salad greens on large salad platter. Using a slotted spoon, place roasted vegetables on top and sprinkle with Parmesan.

Per serving: 202 calories (73 percent from fat), 17 grams total fat (3 grams saturated), 1 milligram cholesterol, 12 grams carbohydrates, 3 grams protein, 81 milligrams sodium, 1 gram dietary fiber.

Shopping Tips: Fresh fennel is available fall through spring. Look for bulbs that do not have any brown spots. If the fronds are still attached, they should be green and fresh.

Salad Boosts Immune System

If watering the houseplants is the closest you get to a leafy green in winter, it's time to rethink your position.

A study in the *Journal of the American Dietetic Association* found that people who eat a serving of salad every day have a much higher likelihood of meeting the recommended dietary allowance for vitamin C.

The Star's Red and Green Salad With Cranberry Vinaigrette features a festive combination of red grapefruit and avocado. An avocado has 20 milligrams of vitamin C, which boosts the immune system, and fresh grapefruit has 48 milligrams. The recommended dietary allowance is 75 milligrams for women and 90 milligrams for men.

Other colorful nutrition benefits from a red and green salad:

Avocados were once considered a dieter's dilemma because of their high calorie count, but new research has given them the green light. Avocados are not only delicious but also contain good amounts of potassium, vitamin A, niacin, fiber and phytonutrients.

Red or pink grapefruit is high in vitamin A, as well as lycopene.

Beets contain potassium, fiber, folate and phytonutrients, including anthocyanins, which give them their deep, earthy ruby color.

To preserve the anthocyanins, it's best to roast, bake or microwave whole beets in their skins; peeled or cut up they lose the beneficial nutrients.

ROASTING BEETS IN A SLOW COOKER:

Trim and peel beet; toss in 2 teaspoons olive oil. Place beet in slow cooker. Cover slow cooker and cook on high setting 3 to 3½ hours or until beet is tender; remove and allow to cool.

Avocado And Grapefruit Salad With Cranberry Vinaigrette

Makes 4 servings

Cooking Tip: When working with beets, you may want to use rubber gloves since the juice can stain.

1 beet, trimmed
1 red or pink grapefruit
1 ripe avocado
1 large head red-tipped leaf lettuce
   or other greens, torn into bite-size pieces
2 tablespoons white balsamic vinegar
2 teaspoons olive oil
1 tablespoon honey
1/4 cup cranberry juice cocktail
Salt and pepper to taste
2 teaspoons minced shallot

Wrap beet in aluminum foil, place in baking dish and bake at 400 degrees 60 to 70 minutes or until tender. Cool, peel and thinly slice.

Peel grapefruit, removing all white pith. Cut along the sides of each dividing membrane, cutting to the core; remove sections over a dish to catch juice. Set aside grapefruit sections.

Peel, pit and thinly slice avocado. Place avocado slices in collected grapefruit juice and toss gently to coat; drain.

Arrange lettuce on 4 salad plates. Top lettuce with alternating slices of beets, grapefruit and avocados.

Whisk together vinegar, oil, honey and cranberry juice cocktail; season with salt and pepper. Stir in shallots.

Drizzle each salad lightly with vinaigrette just before serving.

Per serving: 174 calories (51 percent from fat), 10 grams total fat (2 grams saturated), no cholesterol, 19 grams carbohydrates, 2 grams protein, 24 milligrams sodium, 3 grams dietary fiber.

Enjoy A Salad With Heart

Depending on how you dress it up, a lettuce salad can be ho-hum or ooh-la-la!

The Star's Hearts Of Palm Salad With Remoulade is an example of thinking beyond the typical salad bar standbys.

If you've never tried hearts of palm, the ivory-colored, tube-shaped stalks are the tender center cord of the cabbage palm or palmetto, the state tree of Florida. Hearts of palm can range from pencil thin to 11/2 inches thick, and they taste like a cross between asparagus and artichokes.

Although not inexpensive (depending on size, anywhere from $3.50 to $5 per can or jar), the ingredient can really make a salad special. Look for them in the canned vegetable aisle of well-stocked supermarkets. Nearly half of the hearts of palm imported into the United States are harvested wild from the rain forests of Brazil, but you can also buy cultivated varieties grown in Peru, Costa Rica and Ecuador.

Not to be confused with the highly saturated fat known as palm oil, hearts of palm contain zero fat and cholesterol. They are low in sodium and rich in iron, phosphorous and potassium. A 1/2-cup serving has just 20 calories.

Since the French are hearty consumers of hearts of palm, it makes sense to pair them with a classic remoulade, a sauce made of mayonnaise, mustard, capers, chopped gherkins, herbs and anchovies and frequently served with meats, fish and shellfish. Our version is a delicious mix of light mayo and mustard (a condiment naturally low in calories) with the added flavor and nutrition of roasted red peppers and celery.

Hearts Of Palm Salad With Remoulade Dressing

Makes 4 servings

4 cups spring mix salad greens
1 (14-ounce) can hearts of palm,
    drained and rinsed
1/3 cup roasted red peppers, drained
2 tablespoons chopped green onion
1/4 cup Creole mustard
1/4 cup reduced-fat mayonnaise
2 tablespoons minced flat leaf parsley
1 clove garlic, minced
2 tablespoons chopped celery

Divide spring mix salad greens among 4 salad plates. Chop hearts of palm into 1-inch pieces; place 1/4 of hearts of palm on top of salad mix on each plate, then set aside.

Place remaining ingredients in food processor fitted with a metal blade and process until well-blended. Drizzle evenly over salad greens.

Per serving: 168 calories (18 percent from fat), 4 grams total fat (1 gram saturated), 5 milligrams cholesterol, 34 grams carbohydrates, 5 grams protein, 295 milligrams sodium, 4 grams dietary fiber.

SHOPPING TIP: Creole mustard is available online and in many larger supermarkets. If you can't find it, choose a spicy brown mustard instead.

STORAGE TIP: Hearts of palm should be stored in an airtight, nonmetal container. Refrigerate any leftover stalks in their own liquid for up to a week.

Cooking Tip: Because hearts of palm are cannedin a solution of salt, citric acid and ascorbic acid, it's a good idea to rinse them before adding them to the salad.

Super-Sized Portion Distortion

Photo by Jim Barcus • THE KANSAS CITY STAR

For 30 days documentary filmmaker Morgan Spurlock ate nothing but McDonald's. The resulting Academy Award-nominated documentary "Super Size Me" took an in-depth look at the effects of fast food on American health.

James Painter, chairman of the family and consumer sciences department at Eastern Illinois University in Charleston, is planning his own documentary spin-off. And he's calling it "Portion Size Me."

The gist?

The subjects eat McDonald's, but some super size their portions while others eat a more moderate serving. Instead of a two-fisted, double-decker hamburger dripping with special sauce, why not eat a more modest 3- to 4-ounce portion of lean meat? "People have no idea what a portion is anymore. Portion is key," Painter says.

When Painter asked a formerly overweight man who had lost 95 pounds and kept it off for five years to share his diet secrets, the man said he followed the "Paper and Pencil Diet." He simply wrote down everything he ate each day. By being mindful of quantity, anyone can limit the amount of calories consumed.

The Star's recipe for Grilled Steak Salad With Red Wine Vinaigrette is an example of eating the foods you love but in moderation.

Although eating steaks the size of a hubcap is an American pastime, the proper amount is about the size of a deck of cards or the palm of your hand.

A small portion of beef adds protein to a hearty salad. While we're on the subject, a serving of salad or leafy greens equals 1 cup.

Grilled Steak Salad With Red Wine Vinaigrette

Makes 4 to 6 servings

For the vinaigrette:
6 tablespoons red wine vinegar
4 tablespoons honey
1 tablespoon olive oil
1/4 teaspoon salt
1/4 teaspoon pepper
1/4 teaspoon garlic powder

For the steak salad:
1 beef flank steak (1 to 1 1/4 pounds)
1/2 cup red wine vinegar
1/3 cup ketchup
1 tablespoon Worcestershire sauce
1/2 teaspoon garlic powder
1/2 teaspoon dry mustard
6 to 7 cups torn salad greens
2 cups torn fresh spinach leaves
1 cup sliced mushrooms
1 small red pepper, cut into thin slices
2 Roma tomatoes, chopped

Pump It Up: If sodium is a concern, look for low-sodium Worcestershire sauce, a product that is beginning to appear in supermarkets nationwide.

For the vinaigrette: In a bowl, whisk together all ingredients; set aside.

For the steak salad: Place steak in a zip-top plastic food bag. Combine red wine vinegar, ketchup, Worcestershire sauce, garlic powder and dry mustard; pour over meat, seal bag and refrigerate overnight.

Drain meat and discard marinade. Grill or broil meat, about 13 to 15 minutes or until meat thermometer reaches 160 degrees for medium doneness, turning meat midway through cooking. Allow meat to stand 10 minutes, then thinly slice across the grain.

Arrange salad greens and spinach leaves on serving plates. Top each with mushrooms, red pepper, tomato and meat strips. Drizzle with the vinaigrette.

Per serving, with vinaigrette dressing, based on 4: 353 calories (35 percent from fat), 14 grams total fat (5 grams saturated), 57 milligrams cholesterol, 35 grams carbohydrates, 26 grams protein, 511 milligrams sodium, 4 grams dietary fiber.

Edamame Goes Mainstream

Photo by David Eulitt • THE KANSAS CITY STAR

Got edamame?

Probably not. Just two or three years ago it would have been unlikely that the average supermarket shopper would have been able to find the little green soybeans.

But tastes are changing. Not only is the once-obscure health food readily available in several aisles of the supermarket, it has also hit the big time—as a starring ingredient in McDonald's Asian salad.

Considered a super food, edamame (pronounced eh-dah-MAH-meh) is a high-quality soy food rich in plant proteins; a 1/2 cup has 8 grams of protein. Edamame also contains soluble fiber and plenty of phytonutrients that help maintain low blood cholesterol levels and bone strength and protect against some cancers.

Edamame is delicious steamed, and the beans pop right out of their fuzzy pods. They resemble tiny lima beans and have a delicate, nutty flavor. The Japanese eat edamame as a bar snack and wash it down with beer, but the beans also make a terrific addition to pastas, vegetable salads and grain salads.

The Star's Summertime Wheat Berry Salad With Edamame combines a dynamic duo—edamame with wheat berries, another food poised to enter the spotlight thanks to an increased interest in whole grains. Wheat berries are a pleasantly chewy grain that sometimes show up in pilafs. Like edamame, until rather recently wheat berries also were available only in health food stores.

Wheat berries are whole, unprocessed kernels of wheat. In addition to providing fiber, the kernels contain vitamin B12, vitamin E, protein, essential fatty acids and trace minerals such as zinc, copper, manganese, magnesium and phosphorus. A serving of wheat berries contains 7 grams of protein, more than 20 percent of the recommended daily value of dietary fiber and 10 percent of iron.

Summertime Wheat Berry Salad With Edamame

Makes 8 servings

Shopping Tip: Look
for edamame in
the frozen foods
section of major
supermarket chains.

1 cup wheat berries
3 cups water
1/2 teaspoon salt
1 red pepper, diced
3 green onions, chopped
2 Roma tomatoes, seeded and chopped
1 small cucumber, unpeeled and diced
3/4 cup fresh edamame
1/3 cup chopped fresh flat leaf parsley
2 tablespoons fresh minced tarragon
2 tablespoons lemon juice
2 tablespoons sherry vinegar
1 tablespoon Dijon mustard
1/2 cup plain nonfat yogurt
1 tablespoon olive oil
Salt and pepper to taste

Place wheat berries and water in medium saucepan and bring to a boil. Add salt; cover and simmer for 1 hour, or until the wheat berries are cooked through. (Note: they will remain chewy). Drain and place in large bowl. Add red pepper, green onions, tomatoes, cucumber, edamame, parsley and tarragon. Toss to combine.

Combine lemon juice, vinegar, mustard, and yogurt; blend well. Whisk in the olive oil until blended. Season to taste with salt and pepper. Pour dressing over salad and toss to combine.

Per serving: 195 calories (23 percent from fat), 5 grams total fat (1 gram saturated), trace cholesterol, 29 grams carbohydrates, 10 grams protein, 175 milligrams sodium, 5 grams dietary fiber.

STORAGE TIPS: Refrigerate fresh edamame for up to a week. This salad's flavor gets better with time and holds up well for several days in the refrigerator.

Photo by Tammy Ljungblad • THE KANSAS CITY STAR

Betting On Beta-Glucan

Bets are on that a savvy marketing guru could turn barley into the next oat bran.

In the 1980s, oat bran was the golden child of the grain family, and soon every muffin, cookie and granola bar was sprinkled with the cholesterol-lowering flakes.

Like oats, barley is an excellent source of beta-glucan soluble fiber: 1/3 cup of cooked barley contains 2 grams. Beta glucans can dramatically lower LDL cholesterol and prevent dramatic spikes in blood sugar while promoting a feeling of fullness.

Typically, barley has been used to brew beer and to beef up homey, grandmotherly soups. But with recent FDA approval to make heart-health claims, barley would appear to be poised for a promotion.

A promotion that has yet to come.

"I wish I could tell you there were scores of products (with barley) being developed, but it's not true," says Mary Palmer Sullivan, executive director of the non-profit National Barley Foods Council (barley foods.org).

And don't even get her started about how difficult it can be to even find quick-cooking barley. Spotty availability means it is available in the Kansas City market, but rarely on the supermarket shelves in Spokane, Wash., where she lives.

"When I see it I have to stock up and buy five boxes at a time," Palmer Sullivan says.

The time savings: Regular pearl barley can take 45 minutes to cook, while quick-cooking versions take just 10 minutes. So think of The Star's Quick Barley Vegetable Salad as fast food that's good for your heart.

Quick Barley Vegetable Salad

Makes 6 servings

2 tablespoons butter
1/2 cup chopped onion
1 red pepper, chopped
1 cup sliced mushrooms
1 clove garlic, minced
Freshly ground pepper to taste
1 cup fat-free reduced-sodium chicken broth
3/4 cup quick-cooking barley
1 cup chopped fresh spinach
2 Roma tomatoes, peeled, seeded
    and chopped
1/4 cup minced fresh basil
3 tablespoons grated Parmesan cheese

Melt butter in large saucepan or deep skillet. Add onion and sauté until tender. Stir in red pepper, mushrooms and garlic and sauté until red pepper is tender. Season generously with black pepper. Add broth; heat to boil. Stir in barley. Cover, reduce heat and simmer 10 minutes or until barley is tender and liquid is absorbed. Stir in spinach, tomatoes and basil. Cook, uncovered, 1 to 2 minutes or until spinach is wilted. Spoon into serving bowl and sprinkle with Parmesan.

Per serving: 153 calories (29 percent from fat), 5 grams total fat (3 grams saturated), 12 milligrams cholesterol, 23 grams carbohydrates, 7 grams protein, 181 milligrams sodium, 5 grams dietary fiber.

Cooking Tip: This recipe uses fat-free reduced-sodium chicken broth. It is also good with vegetable broth. But be aware that vegetable broth has more sodium than reduced-sodium chicken broth.

SHOPPING TIP: Quaker Quick Barley was used to test this recipe. If you can't find quick-cooking barley, you may substitute regular pearl barley and adjust the cooking time according to package directions.

In most supermarkets you should find barley with the dry rice and beans, but it may be stocked on the soup aisle.

Add Juicy Fruits To Your Greens

The *Da Vinci Code* isn't the only code worth cracking.

To help more Americans eat the recommended five to nine servings of fruits and vegetables a day, various government agencies have color-coded fruit and vegetables into five color families: green, blue/purple, white, yellow/orange and red.

If you're interested in a comprehensive list, go to www.5aday.org, but rest assured the plot line for produce is really less complicated—and certainly less controversial—than a Dan Brown thriller.

All you really need to remember? The deeper the color, the more bang for your health.

That's because the pigments that give fruits and vegetables color contain antioxidants, compounds credited with preventing premature aging, dementia, blindness, heart disease and cancer.

The Star's Farmers Market Salad combines an impressive mix of summer stone fruit from a wide color spectrum—peaches, nectarines, plums and cherries—served on a bed of seasonal greens. They're referred to as stone fruits because a hard stone pit protects the seed.

Peaches, nectarines and plums contain good amounts of antioxidant carotenoids and vitamin C. If cherries are not in season (look for them in August), try strawberries, which are loaded with vitamin C and potassium. All these fruits contain fiber, particularly if you leave the skin on.

The salad is dressed with a light vinaigrette and sprinkled with toasted walnuts, a nut high in healthy omega-3 fatty acids.

Farmers Market Salad

Makes 4 servings

1/2 cup white grape/peach juice
1 tablespoon white wine vinegar
1 teaspoon walnut oil
Salt and pepper to taste
6 cups seasonal greens, torn into bite-size pieces
2 medium peaches or nectarines, peeled,
   pitted and thinly sliced
1 tablespoon lemon juice
2 medium plums, pitted and thinly sliced
   (peeled if desired)
6 to 8 fresh cherries, pitted and halved,
   or strawberries, halved
1/4 cup chopped walnuts, toasted

Pour juice into small saucepan. Cook over high heat 5 minutes or until juice is reduced to about 1/4 cup. Remove from heat and allow to cool. Stir in vinegar, oil and salt and pepper.

Place greens in salad bowl. Toss peaches or nectarines with lemon juice; drain and add to salad. Add plums and cherries or strawberries. Drizzle with dressing and toss to coat evenly. Garnish with toasted walnuts.

Per serving: 248 calories (23 percent from fat), 7 grams total fat (1 gram saturated), no cholesterol, 46 grams carbohydrates, 7 grams protein, 26 milligrams sodium, 8 grams dietary fiber.

COOKING TIPS: Ever notice how fruits that have been cut tend to brown quickly? When the fruit is tossed with lemon juice, the lemon juice keeps the fruit from oxidizing.

TO TOAST WALNUTS: Place chopped walnuts on baking tray. Bake at 350 degrees about 7 minutes or until lightly toasted.

Shopping Tips: Walnut oil is high in heart-healthy omega-3 fatty acids. Increasingly found at large supermarkets, La Tourangelle is a popular brand. Just remember to go easy: Walnut oil contains 120 calories per tablespoon.

Mediterranean Made Modern

Photo by Tammy Ljungblad • THE KANSAS CITY STAR

For a dozen years, nutrition experts have talked up the Mediterranean diet as the plan for optimum health, and The Star's sunny Greek Orzo Salad pays homage to these delicious, sun-drenched flavors.

More a way of eating than a traditional "diet" plan, the Mediterranean diet is based on the eating patterns of the long-lived people of Crete, the rest of Greece and southern Italy circa 1960. In 1994, the Boston-based nutrition education think tank Oldways Preservation & Trust and the Harvard School of Public Health created a Mediterranean diet pyramid, and, over time, its building blocks have become well-known to the American public:

• Olive oil, a healthy fat, is used as a dressing and a condiment.

• Red meat moves from the center of the plate to side-dish status, while poultry and fish consumption increases.

• Fruits, vegetables, grains, beans, seeds and nuts take center stage.

• Low-fat dairy is OK when consumed in moderation.

• Red wine can be an occasional part of the meal.

Now, there's a new spin-off to the Mediterranean diet. The Sonoma Diet combines the flavor palettes of Mediterranean, Latin and Asian cuisine with the latest nutrition research on portion size, nutrient ratios and phytonutrients.

"This is the first time we've seen nutrition and the culinary arts coming together," says Connie Guttersen, a registered dietitian and best-selling author of The Sonoma Diet (Meredith Books).

A teacher at the Culinary Institute of America's Greystone campus in the heart of California wine country, Guttersen predicts Americans will learn to graze from global menus that offer the hallmarks of the Mediterranean diet—more whole grains, more greens and more fruit desserts—but without the fanfare. "You're going to see chefs cooking with these trendy flavors," she says, "but you're not going to see the little heart signs on menus."

In essence, the Mediterranean diet will have morphed into a lifestyle.

Greek Orzo Salad

Makes 8 to 10 servings

1 cup uncooked orzo
1 red pepper, chopped
1 cup chopped cucumber
3 Roma tomatoes, seeded and chopped
1/3 cup chopped red onion
2 tablespoons sliced ripe pitted olives, drained
2 tablespoons white wine vinegar
3 tablespoons freshly squeezed lemon juice
1 teaspoon grated lemon zest
1 clove garlic, minced
1 tablespoon olive oil
1 tablespoon Dijon mustard
1 tablespoon honey
1 teaspoon sugar
1/2 teaspoon dried basil leaves

Pump It Up: To see the Mediterranean pyramid, go to oldwayspt.org.

Cook orzo according to package directions; drain. Combine orzo, red pepper, cucumber, tomatoes, red onions and olives.

Whisk to combine wine vinegar, lemon juice, lemon zest, garlic, olive oil, Dijon, honey, sugar and basil; pour over orzo mixture. Toss to combine. Cover and refrigerate several hours or overnight. Toss again just before serving.

Per serving, based on 8: 128 calories (17 percent from fat), 3 grams total fat (trace saturated fat), no cholesterol, 24 grams carbohydrates, 4 grams protein, 49 milligrams sodium, 2 grams dietary fiber.

SHOPPING TIP: Orzo, an Italian word that means barley, is actually a tiny, rice-shaped, quick-cooking pasta.

Photo by Tammy Ljungblad • THE KANSAS CITY STAR

Cabbage: Color Your Diet

When it comes to cabbage, think pink.

Cabbage contains indoles, a chemical that can rid the body of excess estrogen, lowering a woman's risk for breast cancer.

In ancient cultures, cabbage was considered a medicine. More recently the National Cancer Institute has found that consuming cruciferous vegetables, including cabbage, may prevent a variety of cancers.

The Star's Wintertime Chopped Salad offers several flavor twists to the typical summer coleslaw.

For instance, chopped celery is a common ingredient, but fennel adds a sweet crunchiness while providing a healthy dose of vitamin A and a fair amount of calcium, phosphorous and potassium. Chopped radishes add a splash of color.

Carrots add still more color and a dash of beta-carotene.

SERVING TIP: Cabbages have great texture, so line the bowl with a cabbage leaf and garnish with roughly chopped pieces.

Wintertime Chopped Salad

Makes 6 servings

1 fennel bulb, trimmed, cut into 1/4-inch slices
    and then finely chopped
1/4 small head green cabbage, finely chopped
    (2 cups, chopped)
6 radishes, finely chopped
2 carrots, finely chopped
1 stalk celery, finely chopped
1/2 cucumber, peeled, seeded and finely chopped
3 green onions, finely chopped
1 teaspoon Dijon mustard
2 tablespoons balsamic vinegar
5 tablespoons extra-virgin olive oil
2 tablespoons finely chopped shallot
Salt and pepper to taste
3 tablespoons fresh herbs such as basil
    and Italian parsley

Combine fennel, cabbage, radishes, carrots, celery, cucumber and green onions in large mixing bowl.

In small measuring cup combine Dijon mustard and balsamic vinegar; stir to blend. Whisk in olive oil until well blended. Stir in shallot.

Pour dressing over chopped vegetables; gently stir to blend. Season with salt and pepper, to taste.

Place in serving bowl and sprinkle with fresh herbs.

Per serving: 139 calories (71 percent from fat), 12 grams total fat (2 grams saturated), no cholesterol, 9 grams carbohydrates, 2 grams protein, 52 milligrams sodium, 3 grams dietary fiber.

COOKING TIPS: To create a confetti of cabbage, you will need a sharp knife. You might be tempted to try cutting down on chopping time by using a food processor, but it can quickly turn your veggies to mush.

Preparation Tips: Cabbage contains plenty of vitamin C, but it begins to lose its potency soon after it is cut, so try to serve it immediately. The other key to a great chopped salad is to finely dice the ingredients so the flavors meld.

Poaching Has A Sexy Sizzle

Photo by Jim Barcus • THE KANSAS CITY STAR

If you were looking for the Rodney Dangerfield of food, poached chicken breasts might top the list.

Next to a sexy little saute, poaching sounds bland. Even though it doesn't get the respect it deserves, poaching is a cooking technique home cooks should embrace.

Because there is no added fat, poaching is a calorie-free way to prepare meats, poultry and fish.

To poach a chicken breast, submerge it in seasoned water and bring it to a boil, then simmer. The cooking liquid will impart a subtle flavor to the finished dish.

The Star's Chinese Chicken and Cabbage Salad recipe calls for poaching boneless, skinless chicken breasts with aromatic garlic, gingerroot and crushed pepper. The chopped chicken is tossed with a pre-pared coleslaw mix, colorful peppers and spinach leaves then mixed with a Chinese-inspired dressing. Topped with toasted almonds, this colorful, crunchy salad would be perfect to serve as lunch or take to a potluck supper.

COOKING TIP: Smooth-skinned and dark green, fresh jalapeños range from hot to very hot. They can also irritate the skin, so you may want to use rubber gloves when handling them. Be sure not to touch eyes, lips or nose.

Chinese Chicken And Cabbage Salad

Makes 6 servings

1 to 1 1/4 pounds boneless, skinless
    chicken breast halves
2 cloves garlic, halved
2 slices fresh, peeled ginger,
    each about 1/4-inch thick
1/4 teaspoon salt
1/4 teaspoon freshly ground pepper
1/4 teaspoon crushed red pepper
4 cups cabbage coleslaw mix
1/2 red pepper, thinly sliced
1/2 yellow pepper, thinly sliced
2 green onions, sliced
1 cup fresh spinach leaves, julienne sliced
Juice of 1 lime
1 jalapeño pepper, seeded and minced
2 tablespoons rice wine vinegar
1 tablespoon reduced-sodium soy sauce
2 cloves garlic, minced
1 teaspoon grated fresh ginger
2 teaspoons sugar
1/3 cup sliced almonds, toasted

To Toast Nuts: Spread nuts in a single layer and toast in a 350-degree oven about 10 minutes. Watch carefully so they don't burn.

Place chicken, garlic, sliced ginger, salt, pepper and crushed red pepper in a saucepan. Add 1 cup water. Cover, heat to a boil, reduce heat and simmer, 15 to 20 minutes or until chicken is fully cooked. Drain and allow chicken to cool slightly.

Meanwhile, combine coleslaw mix, sliced red and yellow peppers, green onions, and spinach leaves in a salad bowl.

When chicken is cool enough to handle, cut into bite-size pieces and toss with coleslaw and vegetable mixture.

Whisk together lime juice, jalapeno pepper, rice wine vinegar, soy sauce, garlic, minced ginger and sugar; drizzle over salad and toss to coat evenly. Garnish with toasted almonds.

Per serving: 162 calories (29 percent from fat), 5 grams total fat (1 gram saturated), 44 milligrams cholesterol, 9 grams carbohydrates, 20 grams protein, 252 milligrams sodium, 2 grams dietary fiber.

Eating With The Seasons

Photo by Jill Toyoshiba • THE KANSAS CITY STAR

A tomato tastes better in summer for one simple reason: It's in season.

There are those who would argue you might be able to get a decent greenhouse-grown tomato year round. But chances are mighty slim that it will taste as perfect as one that has been warmed by the rays of the summer sun.

Eating with the seasons—something most Americans have lost track of—has several advantages: The produce is at its peak of flavor and nutrition, and in most cases it is less expensive. And when you seek out local or home-grown tomatoes, chances are you're also supporting a local farmer, an important consideration since most food travels an average of 1,500 miles from field to fork.

If possible, look for heirloom tomatoes at your local farmer's market. Unlike hybrid varieties bred for shipping long distances, these older varieties have more irregular shapes and come in a variety of colors with lyrical names such as Brandywine, Purple Cherokee and Pruden's Purple. Of course, the beefsteak tomato which is found in most supermarkets is also a fine choice.

I tend to gorge on tomatoes in the summer. I cut way back on my cooking duties, using fresh tomatoes in just about any simple dish, from salsas to salads to pastas. The idea is to create dinners that hardly require more than slicing a tomato. After all, why heat up the kitchen when it's so darn hot outdoors anyway? Plus, if Mother Nature has done her job, the ripe tomato should be able to more than stand on its own.

The Star's Marinated Tomato And Cucumber Salad requires no culinary skills, other than the ability to choose a ripe tomato. Look for vine-ripened tomatoes that are fragrant, firm and free of blemishes. They should be heavy for their size and yield to gentle pressure.

Garnish with cool cucumbers and onions, a food that provides beneficial phytonutrients known as flavonoids and anthocyanins. Drizzle a tablespoon of heart-healthy olive oil over all and garnish with fresh basil and parsley.

Marinated Tomato And Cucumber Salad

Makes 8 servings

3 large ripe tomatoes,
    sliced about 1/4- to 1/2-inch thick
1/2 large cucumber, thinly sliced
1/2 red onion, thinly sliced
1 tablespoon olive oil
2 tablespoons balsamic vinegar
1 tablespoon red wine vinegar
2 tablespoons minced fresh basil
1 tablespoon minced fresh parsley
1/4 teaspoon salt
1/2 teaspoon pepper

Alternately arrange sliced tomatoes, cucumbers and onions in an 8- by 12-inch dish. Combine remaining ingredients, then drizzle over vegetables. Cover and marinate, at room temperature, 1 to 2 hours. (Or if desired, marinate overnight in refrigerator, then allow to stand at room temperature 1 hour before serving.)

Per serving: 32 calories (47 percent from fat), 2 grams total fat (trace saturated fat), no cholesterol, 4 grams carbohydrates, 1 gram protein, 72 milligrams sodium, 1 gram dietary fiber.

Pump It Up: Tarragon, chives and thyme also rev up the flavor of fresh tomatoes.

Photo by Tammy Ljungblad • THE KANSAS CITY STAR

Ginger: Good For What Ails You

When weighing the value of nutrition research, it's important to look at who funded the study.

But in the case of ginger, it may actually be more revealing to know who didn't fund the study.

An ancient food with medicinal properties, ginger contains gingerol, shogaol and zingiberene, which have antioxidant properties. But, says Dana Jacobi, author of 12 *Best Foods Cookbook* (Rodale), "With ginger, there is no one entity that will sit down and say, 'Oh, my! Look at this!'"

And when the research is in, it can take a well-funded marketing campaign to propel a relatively obscure foodstuff into the culinary mainstream.

When studies revealed olive oil was a heart-healthy, monounsaturated fat, the olive oil industry was ready to launch a hefty campaign aimed at American con-

sumers. "From the '80 to the '90s, the olive oil industry spent a fortune to get the word out," Jacobi says.

Even if ginger never commands the research money or gains the mass appeal it deserves, cooks know it costs just pennies to enjoy the rhizome's unique culinary zing. *The Star's* Gingered Carrot Soup combines the exotic spice with the common carrot.

Carrots are loaded with beta-carotene, a pigment found in deep-orange fruits and vegetables. If you're expecting an orange pool in a bowl, the pretty, pastel color that comes from the addition of fat-free milk will be a surprise. (Pleasant, we hope.)

We also sneak in a few parsnips, a root vegetable that is a good source of vitamin C, thiamin, phosphorous, fiber and potassium.

48 Eating for Life

Gingered Carrot Soup

Makes 5 to 6 servings

1 pound carrots, peeled and cut
    into 1-inch cubes
2 parsnips, peeled and cut into 1-inch cubes
1 clove garlic, minced
2 slices fresh ginger, each about 1/4-inch thick
1/2 cup water
3 tablespoons all-purpose flour
2 teaspoons sugar
1/4 teaspoon salt
1/4 teaspoon pepper
3 1/2 cups fat-free skim milk, divided

Cooking Tip:
If a thinner soup
is desired, add
a little more milk.

Combine carrots, parsnips, garlic, ginger and water in a saucepan. Cover, heat to boiling, reduce heat and simmer 20 to 30 minutes or until vegetables are very tender.

Combine flour, sugar, salt, pepper and 1 cup milk in the work bowl of a food processor. Process until totally combined and flour has dissolved. Pour flour-milk mixture into a heavy 4-quart saucepan; stir in remaining milk. Cook, stirring constantly, just until mixture comes to a boil. (Watch carefully so boiling milk does not boil up over edge of saucepan.) Remove from heat.

Transfer cooked vegetables and any remaining liquid to work bowl of food processor. Process until it forms a smooth puree. Spoon puree into hot milk mixture and blend well. Heat, over low heat, just until hot. Ladle into bowls or mugs.

Per serving, based on 5: 188 calories (4 percent from fat), 1 gram total fat (trace saturated fat), 3 milligrams cholesterol, 39 grams carbohydrates, 8 grams protein, 233 milligrams sodium, 7 grams dietary fiber.

PREPARATION TIP: To keep this soup from becoming too frothy, you will need to use a food processor or an immersion blender; a regular blender whips it up until it's foamy like a milkshake.

A Melting Pot Full Of Nutrition

Photo by David Eulitt • THE KANSAS CITY STAR

If America is truly a melting pot, soup often reflects the best flavors of our immigrant cultures.

The Star's Southwestern Black Bean Soup is a fiber-rich soup based on two of the world's most common pantry staples: beans and rice. Beans and rice form a complete protein. When paired with a grocery list of nutrient-rich vegetables, you've got a bowl brimming with good nutrition.

Like wheat bread, brown rice has more vitamins and minerals than white rice. A whole grain, brown rice adds insoluble fiber to the diet and is also an excellent source of manganese, a trace mineral that supports a healthy nervous system. Brown rice is also a good source of selenium and vitamin B6.

Beans are a hearty, non-animal source of protein that can help reduce LDL "bad" cholesterol levels and prevent certain cancers. Beans also help stabilize blood sugars and help dieters feel full longer.

Red peppers add color, texture, flavor and powerful antioxidants, including beta-carotene which protects against certain cancers and heart disease, as well as lutein and zeaxanthin for eye health.

Carrots are one of the richest sources of beta-carotene. A diet high in beta-carotene may cut your risk of cardiovascular disease in half.

Corn provides folate, a B-vitamin that may reduce birth defects, and thiamin, a B-vitamin that helps the body convert food to energy. A deficiency of thiamin results in fatigue.

Fresh salsa adds more vitamins and minerals, as well as flavor to the soup.

Southwestern Black Bean Soup

Makes 10 to 12 servings

1 tablespoon olive oil
1 onion, chopped
3 cloves garlic, minced
4 carrots, chopped
1 red pepper, chopped
1 zucchini, quartered lengthwise and thinly sliced
1/2 cup brown rice
2 (14.5-ounce) cans low-sodium chicken broth
1 (8-ounce) can no-salt added tomato sauce
1 cup salsa
2 cups water
1 teaspoon cumin
1 teaspoon leaf oregano
1/4 teaspoon pepper
1 (15-ounce) can black beans, rinsed and drained
1 cup frozen whole kernel corn, thawed
1/4 cup minced fresh cilantro

Heat oil in a large soup pot over medium-high heat. Add onion, garlic and carrots and saute, stirring frequently, until onion is tender. Stir in red pepper, and sauté 1 minute. Stir in zucchini, rice, broth, tomato sauce, salsa, water and seasonings. Cover, heat to boiling, reduce heat and simmer 30 minutes.

Stir in beans and corn. Simmer 15 minutes, or until vegetables and rice are tender. Ladle into serving bowls and sprinkle each serving with minced cilantro.

Per serving (based on 10): 158 calories (13 percent from fat), 2 grams total fat (trace saturated fat), no cholesterol, 26 grams carbohydrates, 9 grams protein, 230 milligrams sodium, 5 grams dietary fiber.

Pump It Up: Although this soup does not contain meat, canned chicken broth trumped canned vegetable broth because it contains less sodium. If you prefer a vegetarian version, feel free to swap.

Lentils: Packed With Nutrients

A Lenten favorite, lentils have long been served as a low-fat meat substitute.

The lens-shaped legume dates to biblical times. A plant source of protein that cooks quickly, lentils remain an important food staple in many cultures around the world.

Want even more bang for your buck?

Lentils also contain iron, calcium, magnesium, heart-healthy soluble fiber, phytonutrients and folate, a B vitamin that helps the body manufacture blood cells.

Many foods, such as rice, cereals and breads, are fortified with folic acid, but *The Star's* French Lentil Soup is naturally high in folate. For women of child-bearing age, failure to get enough folate can lead to birth defects such as spina bifida. The USDA recommends women consume 400 micrograms of folate a day, and 1 cup of cooked lentils contains 358 micrograms. But everyone—including

PUMP IT UP: To help your body absorb more iron from lentils, eat them with foods high in vitamin C, such as tomatoes, green peppers, broccoli, citrus fruits or juices.

men, the elderly and anyone who suffers from depression—can benefit from more folate in their diets.

"I always recommend eating a source of protein at every meal, and lentils are a great choice. They have B vitamins, lots of nutrients and they're very tasty," says Mitzi Dulan, a registered dietitian and sports nutritionist for the Kansas City Chiefs and Royals.

You can buy dark green French Puy lentils at specialty stores such as Whole Foods and Dean & DeLuca. We paid $8 for 17.5 ounces. Why pay gourmet prices when you can buy a pound of common brown lentils for about $1? Other varieties of lentils such as Egyptian or red lentils popular in Indian cooking tend to fall apart.

French Lentil Soup

Makes 10 servings

3/4 cup cubed lean ham
1 1/2 cups green French Puy lentils
1 cup dry red wine
1 onion, diced
3 stalks celery, finely diced
1 carrot, finely diced
1/2 cup chopped Italian parsley
2 teaspoons dried rosemary, crushed
1/4 teaspoon salt
Freshly ground pepper to taste

Place the ham in a soup pot or Dutch oven.

Add 10 cups water and remaining ingredients.
Bring to a boil over high heat. Reduce heat and simmer 1 hour or until lentils are tender and broth is rich.

Per serving: 149 calories (8 percent from fat), 1 gram total fat (trace saturated fat), 8 milligrams cholesterol, 19 grams carbohydrates, 12 grams protein, 340 milligrams sodium, 10 grams dietary fiber.

Shopping Tip: If you don't have leftover ham on hand, pick some up at the salad bar of your local supermarket.

STORAGE TIPS: Lentils are a great pantry staple. They can be stored in an airtight container for up to a year.

Unlike dried beans, lentils do not need to be soaked in water. Cooked lentils will last up to three days when kept covered in the refrigerator.

Barley Is A Boon To Soups

The Roman gladiators were known as *hordearri*, or "barley men," according to Rebecca Woods, author of *The Whole Foods Encyclopedia* (Penguin/Arkana).

Botanically speaking, *hordeum vulgare*, or barley, was the gladiators' primary food staple. Today most barley ends up malted, in beer or whiskey, or used as animal fodder.

Too bad, because barley's nutty flavor and chewy texture have long made it a tasty addition to breads, cereals and soups in cuisines around the world. But many modern American cooks tend to avoid whole grains such as barley, which requires steaming for up to 45 minutes.

In regional markets where it is available, the "quick" barley featured in *The Star's* Beef and Barley Vegetable Soup is a more realistic option for the time-pressed cook because other varieties, including hulled, hullless and lightly pearled varieties, often require a trip to a natural foods or specialty store. Quick barley has been "pearled"—hulls removed and polished—then steamed and rolled so it cooks in just 10 minutes.

Nutritionally speaking, all forms of barley are comparable in fiber and nutrition, says Mary Palmer Sullivan, executive director of the National Barley Foods Council (www.barleyfoods.org). Unlike other grains, barley retains at least 50 percent fiber throughout the entire kernel, even after the outer bran coating is removed.

One-third cup quick-cooking barley contains 170 calories and 5 grams of fiber. Barley is low fat, has no cholesterol and contains antioxidants, phytonutrients, vitamins and minerals. Barley is a terrific source of selenium, an antioxidant mineral that combines with vitamin E to fight free radicals.

"I think barley has been kind of overlooked for so many years, and we just want to get our time," says Palmer Sullivan. "I think we'll be able to do that with more convenience-oriented products."

Beef And Barley Vegetable Soup

Makes 8 servings

1/2 pound ground round
1 onion, chopped
3 carrots, peeled and chopped
1 potato, peeled and chopped
1 parsnip, peeled and chopped
3 cloves garlic, minced
1/4 teaspoon freshly ground pepper
1 tablespoon dried basil leaves
1 (14.5-ounce) can lower-sodium beef broth
1 (14.5-ounce) can no-salt-added whole tomatoes
2 cups lower-sodium vegetable juice cocktail
1 cup water
1/2 cup quick pearled barley
1 cup frozen mixed vegetables
Hot pepper sauce, pepper and salt to taste

Brown ground beef in skillet over medium high heat; drain. Place in slow cooker crock and add onion, carrots, potato, parsnip, garlic, pepper, basil, beef broth, tomatoes, vegetable juice cocktail and water. Cover and cook on low 7 to 9 hours.

Turn slow cooker to high. Stir to break up whole tomatoes. Stir in barley and frozen mixed vegetables. Cover and cook on high 30 minutes. Just before serving, taste and add hot pepper sauce, pepper and salt to taste.

Per serving: 208 calories (23 percent from fat), 5 grams total fat (2 grams saturated), 22 milligrams cholesterol, 29 grams carbohydrates, 12 grams protein, 72 milligrams sodium, 2 grams dietary fiber.

PREPARATION TIP: If eating well sometimes gets lost in the rush, barley soup may be the answer. It comes together in a slow cooker the night before. Brown the beef and assemble all the ingredients except the potato in a removable slow cooker crock. Cover and refrigerate the filled stoneware bowl overnight.

Shopping Tip: The beauty of soup is that it is flexible and an easy way to introduce an uncommon vegetable, such as parsnip, to your family. Feel free to adjust the vegetables to better suit your family's preference; for example use all carrots and omit the parsnip, or substitute peas and carrots for mixed vegetables.

Casseroles,
Pastas And
One-Pot Meals

French Tradition With A Twist

Photo by Tammy Ljungblad • THE KANSAS CITY STAR

A traditional French cassoulet could never be misconstrued as diet fare.

The white bean stew made from sausages, pork and preserved duck or goose is undeniably tasty but rarely recommended for light eating.

Cassoulet is also a bit of chore to prepare, requiring the duck confit be made at least a week in advance. But *The Star's* version of Winter Chicken And White Bean Cassoulet is as easy on the waistline as it is convenient to prepare.

Substituting chicken breast is a lean option, especially when the skin is removed. But we recommend starting with bone-in breast with skin halves rather than boneless skinless breasts because anything cooked with bone and skin will render a richer flavor.

The size of a lima bean, Great Northern beans add flavor and fiber to the dish. They also are typically grown in the Midwest.

Finally, the flavoring ingredients have been tweaked to heighten the dish's nutrition profile: Fennel is rich in vitamin A and a good source of potassium, calcium and phosphorous; sun-dried tomatoes provide a tart tang and plenty of the antioxidant lycopene; and a splash of orange juice adds flavor with a dose of vitamin C, just the antidote to cold winter days.

PREPARATION TIP: Don't forget to soak beans the night before. Tempted to substitute canned beans for the dry? Convenience comes at a cost, in this case excess sodium. While the fiber content is the same, canned beans that have been rinsed still contain more sodium than dry. Soaking beans isn't difficult; it simply requires planning.

Winter Chicken And White Bean Cassoulet

Makes 6 servings

1 cup dry Great Northern beans
1 tablespoon olive oil
2 medium fennel bulbs (about the size
    of a lemon), each cut into 8 narrow wedges
1 large red onion, cut into 8 narrow wedges
2 bone-in chicken breast halves,
    about 1 1/2 pounds total
1 cup julienned sun-dried tomatoes (dry-pack)
4 cloves garlic, minced
1/2 teaspoon salt
1/2 teaspoon freshly ground pepper
1/2 teaspoon dried oregano
1/8 teaspoon crushed red pepper flakes
1 tablespoon grated orange zest
1/2 cup dry white wine
1 (14.5-ounce) can reduced-sodium chicken broth
3 tablespoons freshly squeezed orange juice
2 tablespoons minced fresh parsley

Shopping Tip: Fennel has an ivory bulb with a feathery green top. In supermarkets it is often incorrectly labeled sweet anise.

Rinse beans and pick over; place in large nonreactive bowl and cover with cold water. Allow to stand overnight. Drain and place in large saucepan. Add cold water to cover beans; heat to a boil, cover, reduce heat and simmer 30 to 40 minutes or until just tender. Drain and set aside.

Heat olive oil in an ovenproof Dutch oven with tight-fitting lid over medium-high heat. Add fennel and red onion and cook 5 minutes, stirring frequently. Remove vegetables from pan and set aside. Add chicken to pan, skin side down and cook until browned, about 6 minutes. Turn and brown on second side, about 4 minutes. Remove chicken and drain.

In Dutch oven, combine beans, vegetables, tomatoes and garlic in pan. Place chicken on top. Add remaining ingredients, except orange juice and parsley. Cover and bake at 350 degrees 30 to 45 minutes or until chicken reaches 180 degrees on meat thermometer and beans are tender. Remove chicken and discard skin; slice meat from bone and return to beans. Stir in orange juice and parsley.

Per serving: 395 calories (11 percent from fat), 5 grams total fat (1 gram saturated), 53 milligrams cholesterol, 52 grams carbohydrates, 38 grams protein, 753 milligrams sodium, 14 grams dietary fiber.

A Lighter Mexican Casserole

Photo by Tammy Ljungblad • THE KANSAS CITY STAR

When Americans eat out, Mexican ranks just behind Italian as our favorite ethnic food. But when we eat in, Mexican is Numero Uno.

Home cooks are making more Mexican, and the cuisine's popularity is up 12 percent since 2003, according to Institute of Food Technologists' report "What, When and Where America Eats."

If you need any more evidence that Mexican has gone mainstream, look no further than the school cafeteria, where sloppy Joes have been edged out by tacos, nachos and fiesta-style pizzas.

The Star's Enchilada Casserole is a Mexican-style family meal with a lighter touch. The recipe starts with a layer of ground round, the leanest ground beef (figure about 11 percent fat). While the lower fat content would produce a dry, tough burger, ground round works well in casseroles.

Corn tortillas also make this casserole a smart choice. Unlike flour tortillas, they do not typically contain added fat, which means fewer calories and more fiber.

Reduced-fat cheese and leaner garnishes, including fat-free sour cream, also boost the dish's nutrition.

PUMP IT UP: Whether eating Mexican at home or ordering it in a restaurant, skip the pre-meal chips and salsa and add a side dish of rice and beans instead. Avocado slices, once thought to be a purely caloric addition, actually add healthy unsaturated fat to the meal.

Enchilada Casserole

Makes 8 to 10 servings

1 pound ground round
1/2 cup chopped onion
4 teaspoons chili powder
1 1/2 teaspoons ground cumin
1/2 teaspoon freshly ground pepper
2 cloves garlic, minced
1 cup water
1 (11.5-ounce) jar mild taco sauce, divided
6 corn tortillas, divided
1 1/4 cups shredded 2 percent sharp cheddar cheese,
    divided
2 green onions, finely chopped
Shredded lettuce, chopped fresh tomatoes
    and sour cream for garnish (optional)

Preheat oven to 375 degrees. Cook ground round and onion in skillet over medium heat until meat is browned and cooked through; drain. Add chili powder, cumin, pepper, garlic and water. Simmer, uncovered, about 10 minutes or until water has evaporated and meat mixture is thick.

Lightly cover bottom of 9-by-13-inch pan with half of taco sauce. Place 3 tortillas in bottom of pan, cutting tortillas to fit, if necessary. Spread meat mixture on top of tortillas. Sprinkle with 1/2 cup cheese. Drizzle remaining taco sauce over cheese and top with remaining 3 tortillas. Sprinkle with remaining 3/4 cup cheese. Cover with aluminum foil and bake 25 minutes. Remove foil and bake 5 additional minutes.

Garnish with green onions and serve with shredded lettuce, chopped tomatoes and fat-free sour cream if desired.

Per serving, based on 8: 253 calories (46 percent from fat), 13 grams total fat (5 grams saturated), 43 milligrams cholesterol, 17 grams carbohydrates, 17 grams protein, 516 milligrams sodium, 2 grams dietary fiber.

Shopping Tip: We used Spanish Gardens brand taco sauce to test this recipe. An 11.5-ounce jar contains 2,600 milligrams of sodium—more than a day's worth of salt. But that is divided among 8 servings, reducing the total sodium to a more moderate 516 milligrams per serving.

Healthy Stew: One-Pot Wonderful

The average American dinner is getting a makeover.

• *Before*: Relying on a hunk of meat as the star of the meal leads to portion distortion, an inability to accurately measure a serving.

• *After*: With the New American Plate, the American Institute of Cancer Research suggests shifting the emphasis from meat to vegetables, fruits and grains—each a bountiful source of phytonutrients, health-promoting nutrients that can protect against cancer.

• *The plan*: Simply fill two-thirds of your plate with vegetables and one-third with meat, poultry or fish.

"People trying to change their diet often get so overwhelmed with counting things," says Karen Collins, registered dietitian and nutrition adviser for the AICR. "The neat thing about the New American Plate is that it does provide structure, but there's not really any counting."

One way to subtly alter lopsided proportions is to serve up more stews, casseroles, stir-fries, grain-based salads and other one-pot meals. *The Star's* Beef And Mushroom Stew is a tasty way to create a quick, convenient and nutritious meal.

Celery, leeks, carrots, mushrooms and peas offer vitamins, minerals and phytonutrients; the small amount of red meat used is lean; and the broth is a low-sodium variety. Serve the meal with cooked brown rice and you've added a healthy whole grain to round out the meal.

PREPARATION TIP: To remove all the grit that can hide in the layers of a leek, slice or chop first, then put in a bowl of water to clean. Swish the pieces with fingers and the dirt will fall to the bottom; lift pieces of leek out with hands. Avoid pouring leeks through a colander, which can trap the dirt with the leeks.

Photo by Tammy Ljungblad • THE KANSAS CITY STAR

Beef And Mushroom Stew

Makes 6 servings

1 1/2 teaspoons olive oil, divided
1 pound beef top round, trimmed
    of all fat and cut into 3/4 -inch cubes
1 onion, chopped
1 leek, chopped (white part only)
1 clove garlic, minced
12 ounces mushrooms, sliced (button,
    small portabella, shiitake or a combination)
2 stalks celery, chopped
3 carrots, halved and sliced
1/2 teaspoon pepper
1/2 teaspoon dried thyme
1/2 teaspoon paprika
1/4 teaspoon salt
1 bay leaf
1 (14.5-ounce) can sodium-reduced beef broth
1/2 cup red wine
1/2 cup frozen peas
1 tablespoon cornstarch
3/4 cup hot, cooked brown rice
Green onions, chopped, for garnish

Pump It Up: For free brochures based on "The New American Plate," go to aicr.org.

Heat 1 teaspoon oil in Dutch oven over medium-high heat. Add beef cubes and cook, stirring frequently, until browned. Drain and set beef aside.

Add remaining oil to Dutch oven. Add onion, leek and garlic and cook, stirring frequently, until onion is tender. Add mushrooms and sauté, stirring frequently, 3 to 4 minutes. Stir in celery, carrots, seasonings, broth, wine and browned beef. Heat to a boil, cover, reduce heat and simmer 1 hour or until beef is tender. Stir in peas. Increase heat to medium. Dissolve cornstarch in 1 tablespoon cold water; blend cornstarch mixture into stew and cook, stirring frequently, about 10 minutes or until slightly thickened and bubbly.

To serve, ladle stew into individual serving bowls. Top each serving with 2 table-spoons hot, cooked brown rice then garnish with green onions.

Per serving: 259 calories (31 percent from fat), 9 grams total fat (3 grams saturated), 36 milligrams cholesterol, 21 grams carbohydrates, 22 grams protein, 194 milligrams sodium, 4 grams dietary fiber.

No Secret To Healthy Chinese

Photo by Tammy Ljungblad • THE KANSAS CITY STAR

Since Nixon's historic trip to China in 1972, the once exotic stir-fry has trickled down to food courts in nearly every shopping mall in America.

Sadly, assimilation has its price.

Although stir-frying has long been revered as a technique that cooks food crisp-tender in a minimal amount of fat, fast-food versions of this dish typically arrive at the table soggy and swimming in a pool of oil. Reasonable portions and a traditionally low meat-to-vegetable ratio are quickly thrown out of balance. And sauces that were once simply sumptuous are transformed into something either cloyingly sweet or loaded with sodium.

What is the best way to control all these factors and still enjoy a healthy stir-fry dish? Make your own, of course. Walk right past the prepackaged stir-fry meal kits in the freezer aisle and go for fresh ingredients instead.

The Star's Beef And Broccoli Stir-Fry offers plenty of nutrition with a modest amount of lean meat and loads of fresh vegetables high in vitamins and antioxidants.

Worried about the prep work? The key to stir-fry success is to prep all the ingredients ahead of time so the actual cooking takes mere minutes. Bonus: Meditative-minded cooks can use the calming, repetitive motion of chopping to relax and unwind in the comfort of their kitchens—no squirrelly teens with boom boxes, unless you invite them.

SHOPPING TIP: For testing purposes, we used Far East brown sauce, a product much lower in sodium than soy sauce: 1 tablespoon brown sauce has just 75 milligrams sodium, compared with 575 milligrams sodium in 1 tablespoon of reduced-sodium soy sauce.

Beef And Broccoli Stir-Fry

Makes 4 servings

2 tablespoons brown sauce
1/2 cup reduced-sodium beef broth
2 tablespoons red wine vinegar
1 tablespoon cornstarch
1 tablespoon reduced-sodium soy sauce
2 teaspoons grated fresh ginger
1/4 teaspoon crushed red pepper flakes
1/2 pound boneless beef sirloin, well trimmed of all fat
    (or ask the butcher to do this for you)
1 tablespoon vegetable oil
1/2 small onion, thinly sliced
2 cloves garlic, minced
1 carrot, cut in julienne strips
1 cup sliced zucchini
2 cups broccoli florets
1/2 red pepper, thinly sliced
2 cups hot cooked brown rice

Combine brown sauce, beef broth, red wine vinegar, cornstarch, soy sauce, ginger and red pepper flakes; set aside.

Slice beef sirloin into 2- by- 1/4-inch strips. Spray a large skillet with nonstick vegetable cooking spray. Heat skillet over medium-high to high heat. Add beef and cook, stirring frequently until browned. Drain and set beef aside.

Heat oil in skillet. Add onion and garlic and cook, stirring frequently, 2 minutes. Add carrots and cook, stirring 1 minute. Add remaining vegetables and cook, stirring frequently, about 4 minutes or until vegetables are crisp-tender. Return meat to skillet and allow to heat through. Push contents of skillet to outer edges of pan. Stir broth mixture well, then pour into center of skillet. Cook, stirring constantly, until mixture thickens. Stir well to evenly coat meat and vegetables. Serve over hot, cooked brown rice.

Per serving, with 1/2 cup cooked brown rice: 308 calories (36 percent from fat), 12 grams total fat (4 grams saturated), 36 milligrams cholesterol, 34 grams carbohydrates, 16 grams protein, 231 milligrams sodium, 4 grams dietary fiber.

Cooking Tip: Although a wok is ideal for cooking stir-fry, any large skillet will do. The secret to stir-fry is threefold: Use high heat, stir constantly and remove the vegetables before they go limp.

A Stew Of Goodness

(B lank) is the spice of life.
Fill in the blank with cloves, oregano, ginger, cinnamon, turmeric, basil, mustard seed, curry powder, paprika, chili powder, parsley or black pepper.

When it comes to health-promoting antioxidants in foods, culinary herbs and spices rank at or near the top of the list.

A study published recently in the *American Journal of Clinical Nutrition* found the 12 spices listed above outranked the more widely touted antioxidant benefits of blueberries, dark chocolate and red wine.

The Star's Curried Pork And Roasted Vegetable Stew is a seasonal dish that takes its cues from several of these heavy-hitters.

Curry powder is a potent blend of up to 20 herbs, spices and seeds such as cloves, cinnamon, cumin, turmeric and black pepper.

Curries get their traditional yellow color from turmeric. The spice also contains curcumin, an antioxidant that may fend off heart disease and cancer.

Paprika is made by grinding sweet red pepper pods into a powder. Chili peppers are rich sources of vitamins A, C and E, folic acid and potassium.

The Romans used cumin as a culinary flavoring and a medicine. Modern scientists are studying it for its possible antioxidant and anti-cancer benefits.

Each of these spices plays well with sweet potatoes and squash, two nutrient-dense vegetables that are, coincidentally, also loaded with powerful antioxidants, especially beta-carotene, a plant pigment that may help prevent certain cancers and ward off macular degeneration, an age-related deterioration of the eye.

SERVING TIP: You can also make these roasted vegetables and serve as a side dish any night of the week.

Curried Pork And Roasted Vegetable Stew

Makes 4 to 6 servings

2 teaspoons olive oil, divided
1 large, sweet onion, chopped
3 cloves garlic, minced
3/4 pound lean boneless pork loin,
   cut into 3/4-inch cubes
2 carrots, sliced
1 teaspoon ground cumin
1 teaspoon curry powder
1/2 teaspoon ground turmeric
1/2 teaspoon pepper, divided
1/4 teaspoon salt
1 (14.5-ounce) can reduced-sodium
   chicken broth
1 large sweet potato, peeled
   and cut into 1-inch cubes
2 cups peeled acorn squash, cut into 1-inch cubes
1/2 teaspoon paprika
1 tablespoon cornstarch
2 tablespoons cold water

Serving Tip: This thick stew would be great served in a bowl, or it could be served over hot, steamed brown rice or in a crusty bread bowl.

Preheat oven to 425 degrees. Heat a large, heavy skillet over medium-high heat. Add 1 teaspoon oil and swirl to coat pan. Add onion, garlic and pork. Cook, stirring frequently, until onion is translucent and pork is browned. Stir in carrots, cumin, curry powder, turmeric, 1/4 teaspoon pepper and salt. Cook, stirring, about 30 seconds or until spices are aromatic. Stir in broth. Cover, reduce heat and simmer 25 minutes.

Place sweet potato and squash cubes in zip-top plastic food bag. Add remaining 1 teaspoon oil and shake to coat evenly. Add remaining 1/4 teaspoon pepper and paprika. Shake to coat evenly. Spread on baking sheet. Bake 20 minutes or until golden, stirring halfway through cooking time. Stir roasted vegetables into stew. Cover and simmer 5 to 10 minutes or until vegetables are tender.

Increase heat to medium. Stir cornstarch into cold water, blending until completely dissolved. Stir cornstarch mixture into stew. Cook, stirring, until thickened and bubbly.

Per serving, based on 4: 261 calories (19 percent from fat), 6 grams total fat (1 gram saturated), 55 milligrams cholesterol, 29 grams carbohydrates, 25 grams protein, 412 milligrams sodium, 6 grams dietary fiber.

Jammin' With Jambalaya

Mardi Gras isn't the only time to savor the joys of jambalaya.

Perfect for a party any time of year, the traditional Cajun-Creole rice casserole is studded with tomatoes, green pepper, celery, onions and bite-size pieces of meat, poultry or seafood.

Although rice is the key ingredient, jambalaya's melodic name may derive from the Spanish word for ham, *jamon*, or the French word, *jambon*.

But there are literally as many recipes for the dish as there are cooks, and modern versions aren't shy about substituting leaner meats, including chicken and turkey sausage.

In addition to choosing leaner meats, *The Star's* Chicken and Sausage Jambalaya adds brown rice to the mix. A whole grain, brown rice retains its high-fiber bran coating.

MAKE-AHEAD TIP: Prepare cooked chicken and sausage as directed. Sauté half the vegetables as directed. Combine cooked meat, cooked vegetables and uncooked vegetables in zip-top plastic food bag.

In a second bag, combine uncooked rice and seasoning. Freeze both bags. When ready to prepare, combine both bags with tomatoes and liquids and bake as directed.

Chicken and Sausage Jambalaya

Makes 10 to 12 servings

2 tablespoons butter
3/4 pound boneless, skinless chicken breast,
    cut into 1-inch cubes
1/2 pound turkey smoked sausage,
    sliced into 1/2 -inch pieces
1 cup chopped onions, divided
1 cup chopped celery, divided
1 cup chopped green pepper, divided
1 tablespoon minced garlic
1 (14.5 -ounce) can whole tomatoes,
    coarsely chopped, do not drain
2 3/4 cups reduced-sodium chicken broth
1 cup uncooked parboiled rice
1/2 cup uncooked brown rice
1/4 teaspoon coarsely ground pepper
1 teaspoon dried thyme leaves
1/4 teaspoon rubbed sage
1/2 teaspoon white pepper

Melt butter in skillet. Add chicken and sausage. Cook over medium-high heat until meat starts to brown. Add 1/2 cup each of onions, celery and bell peppers.

Cook 5 to 8 minutes or until vegetables are tender, stirring frequently. Stir in garlic, tomatoes, remaining 1/2 cup of each raw vegetable and remaining ingredients.

Spray a 9-by-13-inch baking dish with nonstick vegetable cooking spray; spoon jambalaya into prepared dish. Bake uncovered at 350 degrees 1 hour.

Per serving, based on 10: 218 calories (18 percent from fat), 4 grams total fat (2 grams saturated), 48 milligrams cholesterol, 29 grams carbohydrates, 17 grams protein, 488 milligrams sodium, 1 gram dietary fiber.

Cooking Tip: The recipe calls for sautéing half the vegetables, then adding the rest uncooked. The result is a variety of textures in the finished dish.

Rice expands to three to four times its volume when cooked so be sure to use the appropriate size casserole dish.

Quiche Gets A Makeover

Like skirt lengths, quiche has had its ups and downs.

The classic French tart was riding high in the '60s when Julia Child cheered it onto American menus, but by the health-conscious '80s quiche had been declared a dieter's nightmare.

Quiche Lorraine—a sublime blend of cream, eggs, bacon and cheese—contains 40 grams of fat per slice, nearly half of that saturated fat. If you eat an average 2,000-calorie-a-day diet, you've just eaten your recommended saturated fat intake for the day.

The typical pie crust made with vegetable shortening has 949 calories and 62 grams of fat, according to *The Nutrition Bible* by Jean Anderson. *The Star's* recipe for Vegetable Quiche uses phyllo dough, a traditional Greek pastry, to produce a lighter, flakier crust.

Another pitfall is a filling made from cream and whole eggs. Instead, use fat-free milk and pasteurized egg substitute made with egg whites only, which, unlike the yolks, contain no fat or cholesterol.

Skip the bacon and pump up the vegetables. Then try a combination of reduced-fat cheddar cheese and Parmesan, a cheese naturally low in fat. Even if you're not a big fan of reduced-fat cheeses, they work well in casseroles and egg dishes, where they are used as a sidekick, not a star.

STORAGE TIPS: Thaw phyllo in refrigerator. (For this recipe, remove one 8-ounce package; freeze the other for future use.) An unopened package can be refrigerated up to a month; once opened, use within two to three days. Cartons of egg substitute can be refrigerated up to 12 weeks from the date stamped on the container.

Vegetable Quiche

Makes 6 servings

1 teaspoon olive oil
1/2 cup chopped onion
1 cup sliced mushrooms
2 tablespoons water
2 cups chopped broccoli
3 tablespoons all-purpose flour
1 teaspoon dried basil leaves
1/2 teaspoon dry mustard
1/4 teaspoon salt
Freshly ground pepper to taste
1 cup fat-free skim milk
1 (4-ounce) carton egg substitute
1 egg white
1/2 cup shredded reduced-fat sharp
    cheddar cheese
4 sheets phyllo dough
2 tablespoons butter, melted, divided
1 medium, firm, ripe tomato, thinly sliced
2 tablespoons shredded Parmesan cheese

Shopping Tip: Look for phyllo (also fillo or filo) in your grocer's freezer case. Pasteurized egg substitute is available in the dairy case or freezer case.

Preheat oven to 375 degrees. Heat oil in small saucepan. Add onions and cook, stirring frequently, 2 minutes. Stir in mushrooms and cook, stirring frequently until vegetables are crisp-tender. Add water and heat to boiling. Add broccoli, cover and steam 3 minutes or until crisp-tender. Drain well and set aside.

Stir together flour, basil, mustard, salt and pepper in a large mixing bowl. Whisk in milk, egg substitute and egg white. Stir in vegetable mixture and shredded cheddar; set aside.

Spray a 9-inch pie plate with nonstick vegetable cooking spray. Place 1 sheet phyllo in pan, fitting to cover bottom of plate smoothly and folding corners down evenly with top edge of pan. Brush sheet lightly with melted butter. Place a second sheet of phyllo in pan, crisscrossing over the first sheet and folding corners down evenly with edge of pan. Brush entire sheet lightly with butter. Repeat with remaining two sheets of phyllo, adjusting the position so they completely cover the pan, folding corners down evenly with pan and brushing lightly with butter. Spoon filling into crust. Overlap tomato slices on filling. Brush tomatoes and edges of quiche with remaining butter.

Bake 30 to 35 minutes or until almost set and lightly golden. Sprinkle with Parmesan and bake 5 to 8 minutes or until set. Allow to stand 10 minutes before serving.

Per serving: 228 calories (39 percent from fat), 10 grams total fat (4 grams saturated), 15 milligrams cholesterol, 25 grams carbohydrates, 10 grams protein, 436 milligrams sodium, 2 grams dietary fiber.

Prime Time For Swiss Chard

Photo by Tammy Ljungblad • THE KANSAS CITY STAR

Spinach isn't the only healthy green. A worthy substitute? Try Swiss chard.

"If vegetables got grades for traditional nutrients alone, Swiss chard would be the vegetable valedictorian," reports whfoods.com, a nonprofit organization that provides scientific information on foods that promote health.

One cup of Swiss chard is loaded with vitamin K to promote bone health. It's also an excellent source of vitamins A, C and E; iron; calcium; potassium; magnesium; manganese; and dietary fiber.

Wondering how to slip the family some chard?

Chop the leaves of chard, a member of the spinach family, and add them to favorite dishes, including pasta, omelets or lasagna. The tender greens can be prepared like spinach, while the crisp stalks should be chopped, steamed and cooked like asparagus.

Or try *The Star's* recipe for Slow Cooker Risotto With Swiss Chard. It uses a time-saving appliance to make a labor-intensive Italian rice dish with chard, a green available in most supermarkets year round but at its peak in summer.

If you've made risotto from scratch, it is easy to understand why restaurants charge big bucks for a dish made from inexpensive ingredients. The constant stirring required for the grains of rice to absorb liquid is truly labor-intensive.

To get around the labor, dust off your slow cooker and let it cook the rice and greens together into a creamy, one-pot meal.

Slow Cooker Risotto With Swiss Chard

Makes 6 to 8 servings

1 tablespoon olive oil
1 small yellow onion, finely chopped
1 1/4 cups uncooked Arborio rice
2 (14.5-ounce) cans reduced-sodium chicken broth
1/2 cup dry white wine
Dash of salt
1/2 bunch Swiss chard, rinsed clean, well dried and
    coarsely chopped
1/2 cup grated Parmesan cheese, optional

Heat oil in small skillet. Add onion and cook until softened, 4 to 5 minutes.

Place in slow cooker. Add rice and toss well to coat. Stir in chicken broth, wine, salt and Swiss chard. Cover and cook on high 2 to 2 1/2 hours or until all liquid is absorbed. Stir in Parmesan and serve.

Per serving, based on 6, with Parmesan cheese: 219 calories (18 percent from fat), 4 grams total fat (2 grams saturated), 5 milligrams cholesterol, 34 grams carbohydrates, 12 grams protein, 454 milligrams sodium, trace dietary fiber.

STORAGE TIP: Store Swiss chard in a plastic bag in the refrigerator up to 3 days.

Shopping Tips: Look for chard leaves with few bug holes and no yellow spots; avoid limp stalks.

Arborio rice is an Italian-grown, high-starch, short-grain rice that is traditionally used in making risotto because it easily absorbs liquid to give it a creamy texture. Look for Arborio in the rice or ethnic foods aisle.

Riffing On Ratatouille

In the Disney/Pixar movie "Ratatouille," a rat named Remy with a gourmet palate dreams of becoming a great French chef.

The movie takes its name from Remy's signature dish. Pronounced rat-a-too-ee, the Provençal vegetable stew is made from eggplant, tomato, zucchini and green peppers simmered in olive oil and is traditionally served hot or at room temperature, as a side dish or as an appetizer on bread or crackers.

While the movie animators cleverly use a boy-cook named Linguini to camouflage Remy's movements in a restaurant kitchen, *The Star's* Ratatouille With Pasta takes the traditional dish and ladles it over pasta, a kid-friendly comfort food.

The recipe was inspired by Grace Wyss, the 9-year-old daughter of Eating for Life recipe developer Roxanne Wyss. Mom reports Grace was surprised to learn that there was an actual recipe for the movie's famous dish.

COOKING TIP: To peel tomatoes, cut a shallow "X" on the bottom. Place them in a pan of boiling water; allow very ripe tomatoes to stand 15 seconds, firmer ones 30 seconds. Immediately plunge them into ice water.

Photo by Tammy Ljungblad • THE KANSAS CITY STAR

Ratatouille With Pasta

Makes 6 servings

2 teaspoons olive oil
1 onion, chopped
2 cloves garlic, minced
1 1/2 cups cubed, peeled eggplant
  (cut into about 1/2 -inch cubes)
1 small zucchini, chopped
  (about 1 cup chopped)
1 cup sliced mushrooms
1/2 cup chopped green pepper
4 ripe tomatoes, cored, peeled, seeded
  and chopped
2 teaspoons Italian seasoning
1/2 teaspoon sugar
1/4 teaspoon salt
Freshly ground black pepper to taste
2 tablespoons minced fresh basil
8 ounces multigrain penne
  (about 2 1/3 cups uncooked)
1/4 cup shredded Parmesan cheese

Shopping Tip: 1 cup Barilla Plus Penne (uncooked) contains 17 grams protein, 360 milligrams of omega-3 and 7 grams of fiber.

Heat olive oil in 4-quart saucepan over medium-high heat. Add onion and garlic and sauté until onion is translucent. Add eggplant, zucchini, mushrooms and green pepper.

Cook, stirring frequently, 5 minutes. Stir in tomatoes, Italian seasoning, sugar, salt and pepper. Reduce heat, cover and simmer 20 minutes.

Uncover tomato mixture, stir in basil, increase heat to medium-high and allow to boil, uncovered, 3 minutes.

Meanwhile, cook pasta in unsalted water according to package directions; drain. Place pasta in large serving bowl and top with tomato mixture; toss together. Sprinkle with Parmesan.

Per serving: 205 calories (14 percent from fat), 3 grams total fat (1 gram saturated), 2 milligrams cholesterol, 38 grams carbohydrates, 9 grams protein, 159 milligrams sodium, 6 grams dietary fiber.

Photo by Tammy Ljungblad • THE KANSAS CITY STAR

Worldly Cilantro Packs Punch

When it comes to pumping up the flavor of food without adding excess fat and calories, herbs are always a good bet.

One of the most widely used herbs in the world? Cilantro.

Also known as Chinese parsley, the pungent herb packs a wallop to the taste buds but has just 1 calorie per 1/4-cup serving. These tender green leaves are part of the coriander plant and play an integral role in pad Thai, Mexican salsas, Indian raitas, a yogurt-based condiment, as well as Caribbean dressings and marinades.

As cilantro moves into the mainstream in America, it's showing up in new-wave, fusion-style condiments, including cilantro-flavored mayonnaise and cilantro pesto. In addition to its trendy flavor profile, *The Star's* Cilantro Chicken offers the addition of brown rice, a whole grain with lots of fiber.

STORAGE TIP:
Store fresh cilantro for up to a week in a plastic bag in the refrigerator or in a glass of water as you would a bouquet of flowers with a plastic bag covering the top.

Other health benefits? Cilantro is reputed to be an aphrodisiac, an appetite stimulant and a digestive aid. It's rich in vitamins A and C and contains phytonutrients thought to stimulate anti-cancer enzymes in the body.

Researchers at the University of California-Berkeley recently isolated an anti-bacterial agent in cilantro known as dodecenal. Contained in the leaves of the plant, large quantities of dodecenal have been shown to kill salmonella, a form of bacteria that causes food poisoning.

Cilantro Chicken

Makes 4 servings

1 tablespoon olive oil
1 pound boneless, skinless chicken breast halves, cut
    into thin strips
1 tablespoon minced garlic
1/2 cup dry white wine
1 tablespoon butter
1/3 cup chopped fresh cilantro
1/4 cup fresh lime juice
1 tablespoon chipotle chilies in adobo sauce, drained
    and chopped, optional
2 cups cooked brown or white rice
Chopped fresh cilantro for garnish

Heat olive oil in skillet over medium-high heat; add chicken and garlic and cook until chicken is fully cooked and lightly browned. Add wine and simmer 2 minutes. Stir in butter. Add cilantro, lime juice and chilies if desired. Stir in rice. Sprinkle with additional chopped fresh cilantro.

Per serving: 324 calories (26 percent from fat), 9 grams total fat (3 grams saturated), 74 milligrams cholesterol, 27 grams carbohydrates, 29 grams protein, 123 milligrams sodium, 2 grams dietary fiber.

COOKING TIP: Cilantro has an intense (some say "soapy") flavor that can become overpowering if it is added to a dish before it is cooked. It is wise to roughly chop cilantro; minced too fine, it releases the naturally bitter oils of the plant. The tender stems may be eaten along with the leaves.

Cilantro is often used with hot chilies. Chipotle chilies in adobo add optional spice to this dish. Look for chilies in the ethnic foods aisle of your supermarket.

Shopping Tip: Available year-round in nearly every supermarket, cilantro is typically sold in bunches, often displayed near the parsley. Choose cilantro that is bright green and shows no sign of wilting.

Dust Off The Slow Cooker

Photo by David Eulitt • THE KANSAS CITY STAR

Here's a modern tip for cooking more healthful meals: Lean on a time-saving kitchen appliance.

For instance, a slow cooker may be retro, but it can still get the job done. Even on days when your family eats in shifts because of a zigzagging schedule of school activities and night meetings, you can offer something warm, comforting and ready to eat when they are.

Introduced in 1971, Rival's Crock-Pot was the top-selling appliance of its era. With women heading into the workforce in record numbers, 5 o'clock meals à la June Cleaver were disappearing from dinner tables. Desperate for a helping hand in the kitchen, women relied on an arsenal of stay-at-home slow cookers.

On the design side, chrome programmable models have replaced the harvest gold and avocado green Crock-Pots of the past. But there has also been a move to fresher ingredients in the last three decades. My guess is few modern families would be OK with a "lemon" chicken recipe that included lemonade concentrate or a stew that featured onion soup mix and cream of mushroom soup.

The Star's Slow Cooker Chicken And Rice swaps a portion of the white rice for brown rice, in keeping with the USDA's latest advice to consume three servings of whole grains a day for good health. Whole grains provide fiber, vitamins and phytonutrients.

Skinless, boneless chicken breasts have become the ubiquitous choice of health-conscious Americans, but chicken thighs are a tasty and economical choice.

Slow Cooker Chicken And Rice

Makes 6 servings

1/2 cup brown rice
2/3 cup parboiled white rice
1/2 cup chopped onion
1 (4-ounce) can sliced mushrooms, drained
1/2 teaspoon dried thyme leaves
1/2 teaspoon rubbed sage
1/2 teaspoon dry minced garlic
1/2 teaspoon salt
1/4 teaspoon pepper
6 bone-in chicken thighs with skin
1 1/3 cups water
2 tablespoons Worcestershire sauce
1/2 teaspoon paprika
1/2 teaspoon pepper

Spray slow cooker with nonstick vegetable cooking spray.

Spray a skillet with nonstick vegetable cooking spray. Place all rice in skillet and cook, over medium-high heat, stirring occasionally, until rice is golden brown. Remove from heat and stir in onion, mushrooms, thyme, sage, garlic, salt and pepper. Pour rice mixture into slow cooker. Arrange chicken over rice mixture. Pour water over chicken, then drizzle Worcestershire sauce over chicken. Combine paprika and pepper; sprinkle over chicken. Cover and cook on low for 5 hours.

Per serving: 291 calories (46 percent from fat), 15 grams total fat (4 grams saturated), 79 milligrams cholesterol, 20 grams carbohydrates, 19 grams protein, 302 milligrams sodium, 1 gram dietary fiber.

Shopping Tip: Look for parboiled rice in a box rather than a bag. Uncle Ben's patented the process and their labels refer to it as "converted rice," a process that sterilizes the grain.

You Can Bet On Brown Rice

Side dishes can make or break a diet.
So when it comes to making smart choices, a veteran restaurant critic I know offers this rule of thumb: Never eat a starch unless it is "out of the ordinary."

That effectively eliminates most mashed potatoes, french fries, pastas and white rice—largely empty carbohydrates with low nutritional value and just average flavor.

What's left?

Brown rice, whose chewy texture can break up mealtime monotony and boost nutrition.

The USDA recently advised Americans to eat three servings daily of whole grains, which have been linked to a lower risk of cancer, cardiovascular disease and diabetes.

The bran covering on brown rice gives it more protein, fiber and iron than white rice. Brown rice is also higher in trace elements such as selenium, magnesium, potassium and zinc.

"I think people are really hearing the message," says Katie Brown, president of the Kansas City Dietetic Association. "Eat whole grains instead of bread. It's a great, easy way to get fiber."

Brown rice also has more flavor than white rice. "It has that nutty flavor that means you're satisfied more on less," Brown says. "And if you fill up more on sides, you'll eat less of the main entrée, which is usually meat."

The Star's Brown Rice Pilaf takes on a Mediterranean flair after you stir eggplant and cherry tomatoes into the mix. Although eggplant typically soaks up a lot of oil, the recipe achieves a rich taste with only a modest amount of oil.

Brown Rice Pilaf

Makes 6 to 8 side-dish servings

4 tablespoons olive oil, divided
1 small yellow onion, chopped
2 cloves garlic, minced
1 teaspoon ground cumin
1 cup uncooked long-grain brown rice
2 cups water
1/2 teaspoon salt
1/4 teaspoon freshly ground pepper
1 eggplant, peeled and cut into 3/4-inch cubes
2 cups cherry tomatoes, halved
1 to 2 tablespoons Italian parsley, finely chopped
1 to 2 tablespoons fresh basil, finely chopped
2 tablespoons toasted pine nuts

Serving Tip: The total yield on this recipe is adjustable, but keep in mind a serving of rice is 1/2 cup.

Heat 2 tablespoons olive oil in skillet over medium heat; add onion. Cook, stirring occasionally, until onion is softened but not beginning to brown. Add garlic and cumin and cook 30 seconds. Add brown rice and cook over medium heat 3 to 4 minutes or until rice begins to brown slightly. Add water and stir to mix well. Add salt and pepper and bring rice mixture to a boil. Reduce heat, cover and simmer about 40 minutes or until rice is tender and all the liquid has been absorbed.

Meanwhile, in another skillet, heat remaining 2 tablespoons olive oil over medium heat. Add eggplant and cook, stirring frequently until tender, about 10 minutes. Add tomatoes and cook until tomatoes are heated through and liquid has evaporated. Remove from heat and set aside until rice is cooked.

Gently stir eggplant mixture into the cooked rice along with the fresh herbs. Carefully blend ingredients. Sprinkle with pine nuts before serving.

Per serving, based on 6: 251 calories (41 percent from fat), 12 grams total fat (2 grams saturated), no cholesterol, 33 grams carbohydrates, 5 grams protein, 188 milligrams sodium, 4 grams dietary fiber.

PUMP IT UP: Cook the eggplant cubes with the skin on, and you'll retain more water-soluble nutrients.

Hamburger And Plenty O' Veggies

The idea of a skillet supper is hardly revolutionary. A staple in many American kitchens since General Mills introduced Hamburger Helper in the 1970s, the classic casserole was a precursor to today's popular and convenient "meal kits."

The problem with a meal in a box? From a health standpoint, the veggies are dehydrated specks and the powdered seasoning mixes tend to be high in sodium.

The Star's One-Skillet Italian Meal takes a worthy concept and freshens it up: Add sliced mushrooms (buy them pre-sliced in the produce department), green pepper (buy chopped in the freezer case), fresh zucchini, canned tomatoes and fresh spinach.

Finally, substitute Italian vermicelli (ver-mih-CHELL-ee) noodles, literally "little worms," for regular noodles. Vermicelli is thinner than spaghetti, and it's easy to break up the noodles and add them to the pan. They cook through as the meal simmers on the stove-top.

COOKING TIPS: Feel free to substitute alternative vegetable combinations to suit your family's tastes. Instead of 1 cup fresh spinach, try adding an equal amount of chopped Swiss chard, small chopped broccoli florets or frozen peas. Or use frozen spinach, thawed and drained well. Be sure to adjust cooking time accordingly so the vegetables remain crisp tender.

Photo by Tammy Ljungblad • THE KANSAS CITY STAR

One-Skillet Italian Meal

Makes 6 servings

1 pound ground round
1 onion, chopped
2 cloves garlic, minced
1 tablespoon olive oil
1 cup sliced fresh mushrooms
1/2 cup chopped green pepper
1 zucchini, cut into 1/2 -inch cubes
4 ounces dry vermicelli, broken into
   2-inch pieces
3 teaspoons dried Italian seasoning
1/2 teaspoon salt
1/4 teaspoon pepper
1 (14.5-ounce) can no-salt-added whole tomatoes
2 1/2 cups reduced sodium tomato juice
1 cup fresh spinach leaves, coarsely chopped
1/4 cup grated Parmesan cheese

Shopping Tip:
We used
Healthy Choice
reduced-sodium
tomato juice.

Spray a large (12-inch) skillet with nonstick vegetable cooking spray. Cook ground beef, onion and garlic in skillet over medium heat, stirring occasionally, until meat is browned and onion is tender. Drain and set aside.

Return skillet to heat and add olive oil. Add mushrooms, green pepper and zucchini; stir-fry 2 to 3 minutes. Add dry vermicelli pieces. Cook, stirring occasionally and very gently, until pasta is golden-brown and vegetables are crisp-tender. Spoon cooked meat into skillet over pasta and vegetables. Add seasonings, tomatoes and tomato juice. Cover, reduce heat to low and simmer 20 minutes.

Stir in spinach, cover and continue to cook 5 minutes. Sprinkle with Parmesan just before serving.

Per serving: 338 calories (44 percent from fat), 17 grams total fat (6 grams saturated), 55 milligrams cholesterol, 29 grams carbohydrates, 20 grams protein, 324 milligrams sodium, 3 grams dietary fiber.

COOKING TIP: If the kids aren't crazy about tomatoes, use kitchen shears to snip the tomatoes (while still in the can) into small pieces that cook down and nearly disappear.

Evaporated Milk Trims The Fat

A decade ago, the Center for Science in the Public Interest captured headlines when it dubbed fettuccine Alfredo a "heart attack on a plate."

Fettuccine Alfredo ranked fifth on the food industry watchdog's "Hall of Shame" list for restaurant dishes that wreak havoc with a balanced diet.

CSPI found the average fettuccine Alfredo dish contains 1,500 calories, a whopping 97 grams of total fat, 48 grams of saturated fat, including trans fat, a nutritional villain dietitians now recommend we avoid altogether.

Whew!

Despite CSPI's dire warnings, restaurant menus still offer plenty of rich pasta dishes for those who crave the smooth mouth feel of cream. If you share my weakness, *The Star's* recipe for Creamy Chicken Cajun Pasta with a slightly spicy, Alfredo-type cream sauce has just 5 grams of total fat.

How?

One of the best ways to control the quality of the food you eat is to take back the kitchen and cook. Our at-home version is as tasty as any restaurant version, but with a smidgen of the fat found in the original.

The secret ingredient is evaporated skim milk that cooks down to a luscious creamy texture but without the heavy excesses of cream and butter. Evaporated milk has had 60 percent of the water removed and vitamin D added. It also has less fat and more protein and calcium than whole milk but is available in whole, low-fat and skim versions.

The extras?

Parmesan cheese—also high in calcium.

Chicken—a lean protein source.

Squash, peppers and mushrooms, all high in antioxidants.

Finally, the key to making this dish really work for you is to remember to stick with the recipe's recommended serving size. Eating in restaurants can distort our notion of what a plate of pasta should look like.

Photo by Tammy Ljungblad • THE KANSAS CITY STAR

Creamy Chicken Cajun Pasta

Makes 6 servings

3/4 pound boneless, skinless, chicken breasts,
  cut into bite-size pieces
1 tablespoon Cajun seasoning, divided
1 tablespoon olive oil
1 red pepper, cut into thin strips
1 1/2 cups sliced mushrooms
3/4 cup chopped yellow onion
3/4 cup diced yellow squash
2 tablespoons all-purpose flour
3 cloves garlic, finely minced
1/8 teaspoon black pepper
1 (12-ounce) can evaporated skim milk
15 fresh basil leaves, finely minced
8 ounces penne or bow tie pasta,
  cooked according to package directions, drained
1/2 cup grated Parmesan cheese
2 tablespoons coarsely chopped flat leaf parsley

Toss chicken in 2 teaspoons Cajun seasoning. Heat oil in large skillet over medium-high heat. Add chicken and cook until nearly done, about 5 minutes. Add pepper, mushrooms, onion and squash; cover and cook 5 minutes more.

Whisk flour with remaining 1 teaspoon Cajun seasoning, garlic, pepper and milk. Add flour mixture to chicken. Add basil. Bring to a boil and reduce to a simmer, and cook 4 minutes or until sauce thickens, stirring occasionally. (If sauce is too thick, thin with hot water.)

Toss pasta and Parmesan with sauce. Garnish with parsley.

Per serving: 328 calories (15 percent from fat), 5 grams total fat (2 grams saturated), 40 milligrams cholesterol, 42 grams carbohydrates, 26 grams protein, 337 milligrams sodium, 3 grams dietary fiber.

PUMP IT UP: To increase your fiber intake, substitute whole-grain pasta for regular pasta.

Shopping Tip: Do not confuse evaporated milk with sweetened condensed milk, which has sugar added, making it best-suited for desserts.

Photo by Jim Barcus • THE KANSAS CITY STAR

The Magic Of Mushrooms

No wonder Burger King added mushroom burgers to the menu.

Thanks to their deep, earthy flavor, the morsels have gourmet cachet. And new research reveals mushrooms not only taste delicious but also fight disease.

Not a bad marketing strategy.

Scientists have known for years that mushrooms are high in fiber and contain riboflavin, niacin and vitamin B6 that may help fight cancer, heart disease, high blood pressure, high cholesterol and viral infections. Penn State researchers (www.psu.edu/ur/2005/mushrooms.html) recently reported that their more sensitive testing methods found mushrooms are a better source of the antioxidant ergothioneine than either of the previous record holders.

The most commonly consumed white button mushroom has 12 times more of the antioxidant than wheat germ and four times more than chicken livers. A standard 3-ounce serving of mushrooms—about the amount used to top a mushroom burger—supplies 5 milligrams of ergothioneine.

Portabellas and creminis contain even more ergothioneine than white buttons, while exotic mushrooms such as the shiitake contain the most—up to 13 milligrams, or 40 times as much of the antioxidant as wheat germ.

Ergothioneine is not destroyed by cooking, so *The Star's* Mushroom Ragu deconstructs the popular mushroom burger. We saute mushrooms and then simmer them to mimic a traditional ragu, a thick meat sauce that is a staple of Northern Italy's Bologna. For convenience, we've compressed the process by using vegetable cocktail juice as a highly flavorful base loaded with lycopene, an antioxidant that is especially high in cooked tomato sauces.

Mushroom Ragu

Makes 6 servings

1 tablespoon olive oil
1 pound mixed mushrooms, including
    white button, baby bella and shiitake,
    coarsely diced
1 cup chopped yellow onion
1 pound ground round,
    browned and drained
1 (46-ounce) bottle lower-sodium
    vegetable juice cocktail
1 (6-ounce) can tomato paste
1 teaspoon sugar
1/2 teaspoon coarsely ground black pepper
1/2 teaspoon dried minced garlic
1 teaspoon dried basil
2 teaspoons Worcestershire sauce
12 ounces no-yolk egg noodles, cooked
    according to package directions, or
    6 thick-cut slices toasted sourdough bread
Reduced-fat or no-fat sour cream for garnish,
    optional

Shopping Tip: We used three common mushroom types available in most supermarkets. If you can't find one type at your store, feel free to substitute another.

Heat olive oil in Dutch oven over medium-high heat. Add mushrooms and onions and saute until onions are tender and mushrooms have cooked away most of the liquid. Add remaining ingredients except noodles and sour cream. Simmer 30 to 40 minutes, stirring occasionally.

Divide noodles or bread among 6 shallow rimmed bowls. Top with ragu and dollop with sour cream.

Per serving: 605 calories (27 percent from fat), 17 grams total fat (6 grams saturated), 52 milligrams cholesterol, 72 grams carbohydrates, 31 grams protein, 366 milligrams sodium, 8 grams dietary fiber.

STORAGE TIP: Although the cultivated varieties are usually sold in packages wrapped in cellophane, fresh mushrooms need cool air to circulate around them. When you get them home, unwrap and place them on a tray in a single layer. Covered with a damp towel, mushrooms will keep in the refrigerator up to three days. Before adding them to a recipe, wipe the caps and stems with a damp paper towel. Never soak mushrooms in water or they will become mushy.

A Truce In The Carb Wars

In the Atkins era, a plate of pasta was considered an evil entrée.

But with the USDA's new emphasis on whole grains, noodles made from whole wheat, buckwheat, quinoa and spelt are moving to the center of the plate.

A diet rich in whole grains reduces the risk of diabetes, heart disease and cancer, yet the USDA reports only 7 percent of Americans eat the recommended three servings a day, while 42 percent eat no whole grains at all.

Until recently whole grains made up only 10 percent of the typical supermarket, according to the Whole Grains Council (www.wholegrainscouncil.org). In the last year, bread bakers and pasta/cereal/snack makers have added more whole-grain or multigrain products to supermarket shelves.

SHOPPING TIP:

For testing purposes, we used Heartland Multi Grain rotini made by American Italian Pasta Co. The Kansas City-based company is the largest producer and packager of dry pasta in North America.

Once considered chewier and grittier than traditional pastas made with refined white flour, the newly reformulated versions generally have a lighter, nuttier, less-gummy flavor. In some cases, cooking times have been reduced.

Nutritionally speaking, whole-grain pasta has 25 percent more protein and at least three times more fiber.

For *The Star's* Multigrain Pasta Tuna Salad, we used a multigrain rotini with 5 grams of dietary fiber per serving. Additional ingredients boost the recipe to 7 grams per serving.

The pasta salad is tossed with water-packed tuna, an excellent source of omega-3; antioxidant-rich red peppers; and artichokes, a source of vitamin A.

Multigrain Pasta Tuna Salad

Makes 6 servings

2 cups multigrain rotini
1 (9-ounce) package frozen artichoke hearts
1/2 cup sliced celery
3 tablespoons chopped fresh basil
1 (12-ounce) can solid white albacore tuna packed in water, drained
1 (7.25-ounce) jar roasted red peppers, drained and coarsely chopped
1/2 cup fat-free peppercorn ranch dressing
1/3 cup dry roasted cashews or peanuts
Romaine leaves, optional

Cook pasta according to package directions; drain and rinse with cold water. Place pasta in large bowl.

Place artichoke hearts in microwave-safe bowl; cover and microwave on high (100 percent) power 4 minutes. Place cooked artichoke hearts on paper towels to drain well. Coarsely chop, then add to pasta. Add remaining ingredients, except cashews and romaine leaves. Cover and chill for several hours.

To serve, line bowls with romaine leaves if desired; spoon salad over lettuce. Sprinkle with cashews or peanuts.

Per serving: 266 calories (17 percent from fat), 5 grams total fat (1 gram saturated), 17 milligrams cholesterol, 34 grams carbohydrates, 21 grams protein, 432 milligrams sodium, 7 grams dietary fiber.

COOKING TIP: The cooking time for this multigrain pasta is just 6 to 8 minutes, comparable to conventional white pasta. Be sure to read the label and cook according to package directions.

Serving Tip: With pasta, portion size is often difficult to judge. One serving is 1/2 cup, cooked, or about the size of a baseball.

Priceless End-Of-Summer Taste

Photo by Tammy Ljungblad • THE KANSAS CITY STAR

The fewer ingredients in a recipe, the higher their quality must be.

The Star's recipe for Fresh Heirloom Tomatoes With Spaghetti is a case in point. Theoretically, you could make this recipe using any old flavorless tomato picked while barely ripe, but why bother?

If it's flavor you seek, make this recipe when the locally grown tomato crop is in season. The best time to enjoy tomatoes is mid-June through mid-September.

Unless you grow your own, be on the lookout for heirloom varieties available at farmers markets or upscale supermarkets.

Bred for flavor rather than supermarket aesthetics and long-distance shipping requirements, heirlooms come in a rainbow of colors and a variety of lopsided shapes. Most also have fun names, such as Mortgage Lifter, Cherokee Purple and Green Zebra, and are highly perishable.

Heirloom tomatoes tend to be pricey. But after splurging intermittently on these beauties, I think their overall taste and eye appeal make them worth the added expense in a dish where they have a starring role.

Nutritionally speaking, tomatoes are an excellent source of the antioxidant lycopene. Studies have shown lycopene can help prevent heart disease and some cancers, especially prostate cancer.

Vine-ripened tomatoes contain more lycopene than those picked while still green and allowed to ripen off the vine.

Tomatoes taste great with extra-virgin olive oil, a heart-healthy fat, which, coincidentally, makes the lycopene more available to the body.

Tomatoes contain a good amount of vitamin C, which can be lost when they are processed.

Fresh Heirloom Tomatoes With Spaghetti

Makes 6 servings

1 1/2 to 2 pounds tomatoes, chopped
1/2 cup finely chopped onion
2 cloves garlic, minced
1 tablespoon dried basil leaves
3 tablespoons extra-virgin olive oil
Salt and pepper to taste
1 (12-ounce) package multigrain spaghetti
1/2 cup shredded Parmesan cheese

Storage Tip: Never refrigerate whole tomatoes, which can ruin their flavor. Do refrigerate leftover pasta.

Combine tomatoes, onion, garlic, basil, olive oil, salt and pepper in large bowl. Cover with plastic wrap and allow to stand at room temperature 1 to 2 hours.

Cook spaghetti according to package directions; drain and toss with tomato mixture. Sprinkle with Parmesan.

Per serving: 315 calories (26 percent from fat), 10 grams total fat (2 grams saturated), 5 milligrams cholesterol, 49 grams carbohydrates, 12 grams protein, 128 milligrams sodium, 6 grams dietary fiber.

SHOPPING TIP: This recipe was tested using Heartland Multi Grain spaghetti made from whole-grain wheat, brown rice, oats and wheat bran to test this recipe. A 2-ounce serving has 5 grams of fiber.

Go For Guilt-Free Pesto

If your slumbering taste buds are revved up and ready for a taste of summer, you can't go wrong with a dollop of basil pesto.

Except, of course, if you're counting calories.

An uncooked Italian sauce from Genoa, pesto is traditionally made from fresh basil, toasted pine nuts, Parmesan or pecorino cheese and olive oil. Whether pounded with a mortar and pestle or whirred in a food processor, the resulting green slurry is typically mixed with pasta.

In recent years, it has become a supermarket staple. Every bit as popular as marinara or Alfredo sauce, pesto has "one enormous shortcoming...: It oozes fat," writes Jean Anderson, author of *The Nutrition Bible* (Morrow).

PUMP IT UP: To add fiber, try using whole-grain pasta.

Sure, olive oil is a "good" monounsaturated fat. But Anderson makes an important point. Before slathering it on with wild abandon, it's important to keep in mind that olive oil contains 120 calories per tablespoon—not exactly diet fare.

Some recipes try to reduce the oil by adding broth. But *The Star's* Healthy Basil Pesto Pasta adds a fresh, juicy tomato instead, and no one at my house was the wiser. Our sleight of hand punches up the nutrition further by adding a bit of lycopene to the basil, which is loaded with antioxidants that can reduce harmful LDL cholesterol and suppress tumor growth.

Healthy Basil Pesto Pasta

Makes 8 side-dish servings

2 cups fresh basil leaves
1 to 2 cloves garlic, halved
3 tablespoons pine nuts, toasted
2 tablespoons extra-virgin olive oil
1 medium tomato, peeled and seeded
1/3 cup shredded Parmesan cheese
Salt and pepper to taste
12 ounces cooked pasta such as penne
    or cavatappi, drained

Place basil, garlic and pine nuts in bowl of food processor. Pulse to blend; using rubber scraper, scrape down sides of the work bowl. With food processor running, slowly add olive oil until blended. Add tomato; pulse to blend. Remove to bowl and add Parmesan and salt and pepper, to taste. Toss with hot pasta.

Per serving: 219 calories (25 percent from fat), 6 grams total fat (1 gram saturated), 2 milligrams cholesterol, 33 grams carbohydrates, 8 grams protein, 58 milligrams sodium, 2 grams dietary fiber.

Shopping Tips: The recipe calls for close to 2 cups of basil leaves. Granted, it's not inexpensive to buy basil out of season, but I guarantee it's a whole lot better than the gloppy, store-bought containers of the stuff that may contain less expensive walnuts and a lower grade of olive oil.

COOKING TIPS: Submerge tomato in boiling water for 15 to 30 seconds to make it easier to peel.

The amount of garlic you use is a personal choice, but it does contain allicin, a phytonutrient that has antibacterial properties.

STORAGE TIP: As the farmers markets begin to offer fresh basil, buy it in bunches. Make the pesto without the cheese and freeze it in an ice cube tray; pop out the cubes and store for up to three months. When thawed, stir in cheese.

If you have extra pesto left, use it on grilled chicken or fish.

Meat,
Seafood And
Fish Dishes

3

Small Fowl Is Just The Right Size

When it comes to keeping portion sizes in check, Cornish hens are a shoo-in.

A hybrid between Cornish and White Rock chickens, the resulting miniature poultry typically weighs just 1 to 2 pounds, enough to serve two people.

The Cornish hens (also referred to as Rock Cornish game hens) arrived on the scene in 1965 and were first marketed as a gourmet food by Tyson. While they continue to make an elegant presentation for entertaining, there's no reason not to serve the roasted hens for a weeknight meal.

Just think of the hens as you would a little chicken, or for that matter as a teeny-tiny turkey. Either way, the roasting procedure is the same and because they're so small, dinner is ready in an hour.

The Star's recipe for Cornish Hens In Cider is low in sodium and high in protein. Although the total fat content is high, the amount of saturated fat is moderate. The cider keeps the lean (mostly breast) meat on the bird moist. The apples give the hens a seasonal spin while boosting the antioxidants and fiber content of the meal.

TO SERVE: After roasting, allow hen to stand 10 minutes. Pull leg away with a carving fork and, using a sharp knife, cut through to detach the leg and thigh. Repeat on other side. Cut straight down along one side of breast bone to carve off the remaining meat.

Photo by Tammy Ljungblad • THE KANSAS CITY STAR

Cornish Hens In Cider

Makes 4 servings

1/2 lemon, cut into two pieces
2 Cornish hens (18 ounces each)
2 teaspoons olive oil
Salt and freshly ground pepper to taste
3 shallots, peeled and sliced very thin
3 large apples, such as Fuji or Golden Delicious
1/2 teaspoon dried thyme
3/4 cup apple cider
1/4 cup water

Preheat oven to 375 degrees. Squeeze a lemon quarter into each cavity and place the quarter in hen. Rub olive oil over each hen. Season with salt and pepper. Secure Cornish hen with string and tuck wings underneath.

Place in deep skillet or roasting pan. Sprinkle the shallots around the hens. Peel and core the apples and cut into thick slices. Place the apple pieces around hens. Sprinkle thyme over all ingredients. Pour cider and water over all. Roast 55 to 65 minutes or until meat reaches 180 degrees.

Carve hens in half and discard lemons. Serve with apples and shallots. Pour some pan juice over the top.

Per serving: 432 calories (36 percent from fat), 18 grams total fat (4 grams saturated), 105 milligrams cholesterol, 53 grams carbohydrates, 19 grams protein, 66 milligrams sodium, 8 grams dietary fiber.

COOKING TIPS: For a thicker sauce, remove apples and shallots from pan juices and simmer liquid until it is reduced by about half. Chefs typically call this a reduction and it concentrates the cider flavor.

Shopping Tip: Look for Cornish hens in the freezer case. Buy without giblets if possible and be sure to leave the birds in the refrigerator to defrost the night before you plan to make this recipe.

Skinny Dipping In White Sauce

In the Midwest, barbecue sauce is red. But in northern Alabama, white sauce rules.

Barbecue lore offers this nugget: In 1925, a 6-foot-4-inch, 300-pound railroad worker-turned-pitmaster named Big Bob Gibson from Decatur, Ala., began using a rather thin vinegar-mayonnaise sauce flecked with black pepper to marinate his chicken.

Today his offspring carries on the white sauce tradition at Big Bob Gibson Bar-B-Q restaurants. According to the restaurant's Web site, www.big-bobgibsonbbq.com, whole chickens are split, seasoned and laid open on the hickory-smoke pit to cook at 350 degrees for 3 1/2 hours. Just before serving, the birds get a dip in a vat of white sauce.

"I thought it would have a more mayonnaise-y accent, but the first thing I think of is vinegary," says Ardie Davis, a Kansas City-based barbecue sauce expert and the author of The Great BBQ Sauce Book (Ten Speed Press).

"It's also good on pork because it complements the natural sweetness of the meat. What I regret is in Kansas City you just can't go to the store and buy it."

Order a case of Big Bob's White Sauce off the Internet and it will set you back $30, plus shipping and handling. But if you're not sure you're ready to wholesale switch from red to white, The Star's recipe for Grilled Chicken With Alabama White Sauce lets you make a homemade version—one that will also save on fat and calories.

Anyone looking for balance in their diet knows mayonnaise is not a condiment you want to overdo: 1 tablespoon has 103 calories and almost 12 grams of fat versus a reduced-fat version, which has about 49 calories and less than 5 grams of fat, according to the USDA Nutrient Database.

Instead of slow cooking a whole bird, we opted for boneless, skinless chicken breast on the grill, which cuts down on cooking time, as well as reducing portion size and total amount of fat.

Grilled Chicken With Alabama White Sauce

Makes 4 servings

1/4 teaspoon garlic powder
1/2 teaspoon paprika
1/4 teaspoon chili powder
Dash of salt
4 boneless, skinless chicken breast halves
1/2 cup reduced-fat mayonnaise
1/3 cup cider vinegar
1 tablespoon coarsely ground black pepper
Dash of hot pepper sauce
Dash of salt
1 teaspoon lemon juice

Combine garlic powder, paprika, chili powder and salt. Rinse chicken breasts and pat dry; rub seasoning mixture evenly over both sides of chicken.

Preheat grill or allow coals to burn down to white ash. Grill chicken 9 to 12 minutes, until fully cooked and meat thermometer registers 170 degrees, turning midway through cooking.

Combine remaining ingredients and whisk until smooth. Serve sauce spooned over grilled chicken or serve as a dipping sauce.

Per serving: 214 calories (41 percent from fat), 10 grams total fat (1 gram saturated), 76 milligrams cholesterol, 5 grams carbohydrates, 26 grams protein, 285 milligrams sodium, 1 gram dietary fiber.

COOKING TIP: If your chicken breasts are larger than a deck of cards (3 to 4 ounces), trim to the appropriate size.

Pump It Up: For added nutrition, serve wilted collard greens, Swiss chard or spinach. If you have leftover white sauce, use it as a dressing for coleslaw.

Time To Talk Turkey

Turkey. It's not just for Thanksgiving.

Ground turkey burgers have been a staple for health-conscious Americans in recent years. But this summer new cuts of turkey are landing on the grill.

The Star's recipe for Citrus Glazed Turkey With Spicy Pineapple-Orange Marmalade uses lean cutlets, a smaller, flatter cut than tenderloin. A 3-ounce serving of boneless, skinless turkey breast cutlet contains 120 calories, 26 grams of protein, 1 gram of fat and 0 grams of saturated fat, according to the National Turkey Federation.

Of course, the leaner the meat, the more chance there is of it drying out during cooking. To avoid this, a low-fat marinade helps the meat retain moisture.

Go ahead and skip the predictable cranberry sauce. Like cranberries, pineapple has both an astringency and sweetness that complements the neutral flavor of turkey.

Pineapple also contains bromelain, an anti-inflammatory enzyme that may lower the risk of heart attack and stroke, and manganese, an important bone-building mineral. Heating pineapple makes the soluble fiber more available for use by the body.

Citrus Glazed Turkey With Spicy Pineapple Orange Marmalade

Makes 6 servings

1/2 cup orange juice
1/4 cup lime juice
Grated zest of 1 orange
Grated zest of 1 lime
1 clove garlic, minced
1 jalapeño pepper, seeded and minced
1 tablespoon vegetable oil
1 1/2 pounds turkey breast cutlets,
    each cut about 1/2-inch thick
1 tablespoon honey
1/2 cup chopped red onion
1 (8-ounce) can crushed pineapple in juice,
    drained, reserving juice

Shopping Tip: If you can't find cutlets, buy a tenderloin and cut it across the grain to create your own cutlets.

Combine juices, zests, garlic and jalapeño pepper. Measure out about half of juice mixture; cover and refrigerate. Mix oil into remaining juice mixture. Place turkey in zip-top plastic bag. Pour juice mixture over turkey; seal and refrigerate several hours or overnight.

Preheat grill or allow coals to burn down to white ash. Grill turkey about 7 to 8 minutes per side, or until meat is no longer pink and meat thermometer registers 180 degrees. (Do not overcook.)

Meanwhile place reserved juice mixture in small saucepan. Stir in honey, onion and pineapple juice. Heat, stirring frequently, until mixture boils. Reduce heat and simmer, uncovered, about 15 minutes until juice has reduced to about half of original volume. Stir in pineapple and heat, stirring frequently, 2 to 3 minutes. Serve turkey with warm pineapple mixture.

Per serving: 252 calories (37 percent from fat), 10 grams total fat (2 grams saturated), 74 milligrams cholesterol, 14 grams carbohydrates, 25 grams protein, 68 milligrams sodium, 1 gram dietary fiber.

COOKING TIP: To put some handsome crisscross grill marks on your cutlet, position meat at 10 o'clock on the grill. Halfway through cooking time, use a spatula to reposition cutlet at 2 o'clock; flip on the other side and repeat.

Italian Mainstay Gets A Remake

Photo by Tammy Ljungblad • THE KANSAS CITY STAR

Whether you order chicken spiedini at an Italian mom-and-pop ristorante or the Olive Garden, chances are good the benefits of grilling lean chunks of meat over an open flame will be overshadowed by the dish's overall fat content.

The culprit?

Typically the skewered, breaded kebabs are served drowning in a puddle of olive oil. For instance, one recipe on cdkitchen.com calls for 1/2 cup olive oil. Another on recipezaar.com lists 2 tablespoons olive oil and 2 tablespoons butter.

The Star's Grilled Chicken Spiedini adds more zesty lemon and spicy pepperoncini, a mixture that balances flavor with a more modest tablespoon of olive oil.

SERVING TIP: Instead of serving the grilled chicken over a bed of fettuccine Alfredo—referred to by the Center for Science in the Public Interest as a "heart attack on a plate"—try it on a bed of noodles lightly dressed in the pepperoncini sauce plus a dab of heart-healthy olive oil, if desired.

Grilled Chicken Spiedini

Makes 4 servings

1/2 cup lemon juice
3 tablespoons grated lemon zest, divided
1 tablespoon olive oil
2 tablespoons chopped pickled pepperoncini
4 boneless, skinless chicken breast halves
2/3 cup Italian seasoned bread crumbs
1/3 cup grated Parmesan cheese
1 tablespoon chopped parsley
2 garlic cloves, minced

Combine lemon juice, 1 tablespoon lemon zest and olive oil; blend well. Remove 2 tablespoons lemon juice mixture, stir in pepperoncini and set aside. Place remaining mixture into zip-top plastic bag and add chicken breasts. Seal bag, refrigerate and allow to marinate 30 minutes.

Place bread crumbs, Parmesan, parsley, remaining 2 tablespoons lemon zest and garlic cloves in shallow dish such as a pie plate; blend well. Remove each chicken breast from marinade and place in crumb mixture, coating well. Carefully cut each breast into 1-inch thick slices and thread onto metal skewers.

Preheat grill to medium-high (400 degrees, see Grilling Tip) allowing coals to burn down to white ash. Grill chicken 9 to 12 minutes, or until fully cooked and meat thermometer registers 170 degrees, turning midway through cooking.

Place on serving platter and drizzle with pepperoncini mixture.

Per serving: 275 calories (24 percent from fat), 7 grams total fat (2 grams saturated), 71 milligrams cholesterol, 19 grams carbohydrates, 32 grams protein, 489 milligrams sodium, 2 grams dietary fiber.

GRILLING TIP: At 400 degrees, you should be able to hold your hand 4 inches above the grate and count to four, using the "1 Mississippi, 2 Mississippi…" method, before the heat forces you to pull it away.

Shopping Tip: Look for pickled pepperoncini in the condiment aisle with salad dressings, pickles and peppers. You can also find them on some salad bars.

Splurge Once In A While

If you're trying to eat more healthfully or shed a few pounds, it's easy to forget food is more than fuel.

Food is history, family, love and caring, too. Depriving yourself of flavors you enjoy is only likely to make you binge unless you can find balance. So keeping a slightly decadent dish in your repertoire to pull out for special occasions or a night of entertaining is actually a smart idea.

Regular readers will notice that *The Star's* recipe for Chicken With Romesco-Style Sauce is higher in fat and calories than most dishes that appear in this column. Generally, we try to keep a dish between 20 percent and 35 percent fat. Still, our version cuts down on the amount of fat and calories found in traditional romesco recipes.

And, it tastes fabulous.

Romesco is a classic sauce from the Catalonia region of Spain made of finely ground tomatoes, red

SHOPPING TIP: Depending on where you shop, look for panko in the following aisles: breadings and coatings aisle, in the ethnic aisle or in the bread aisle.

bell peppers, garlic, toasted almonds, parsley and olive oil. All these ingredients are considered good nutrition choices, adding phytonutrients from the vegetables, "good" monounsaturated fats from the olive oil, omega-3 fatty acids from the almonds for loads of flavor.

The chicken in this dish is breaded with panko, a Japanese bread crumb that is lighter than the typical American-style bread crumb coatings. Combined with the low-fat buttermilk, panko creates a light, crunchy crust that envelopes the meat.

Chicken With Romesco-Style Sauce

Makes 4 servings

4 Roma tomatoes
2 (1-inch thick) slices baguette, toasted
2 cloves garlic, cut in half
1/3 cup sliced almonds, toasted
1/2 teaspoon crushed red pepper flakes
3/4 cup bottled roasted red peppers, drained
1/4 cup Italian parsley
2 tablespoons sherry vinegar
1/4 cup extra-virgin olive oil
Salt and pepper to taste
1 tablespoon olive oil
1 cup low-fat buttermilk
1 1/2 cups panko crumbs
    or fresh baguette crumbs
4 (4- to 6-ounce) boneless, skinless
    chicken breast halves

Storage Tip: If sauce is left over serve with roasted vegetables for an excellent presentation. It's also good served on grilled fish or poultry.

Preheat broiler. Slice tomatoes in half lengthwise and place on baking sheet. Broil 2 to 4 minutes until charred on one side. Turn and broil an additional 2 to 4 minutes until charred. Transfer to plate and allow to cool.

Place toasted bread, garlic, almonds and pepper flakes in work bowl of food processor. Pulse to form a paste. Peel and core tomatoes and add to food processor along with roasted red peppers, parsley and vinegar. Process and with the machine running add 1/4 cup extra-virgin olive oil in a slow, steady stream. Scrape bowl and add salt and pepper. Allow sauce to stand at room temperature while preparing chicken.

Heat 1 tablespoon olive oil in large skillet that has been sprayed with nonstick vegetable cooking spray over medium-high heat. Place buttermilk in shallow pie plate and place panko crumbs in shallow pie plate. Pound chicken until 1/4-inch thick. Dip chicken in buttermilk, then in bread crumbs; place in hot skillet and saute until browned; turn and brown other side and cook until fully cooked and meat thermometer registers 170 degrees. Serve cooked chicken with Romesco sauce.

Per serving: 468 calories (50 percent from fat), 26 grams total fat (4 grams saturated), 67 milligrams cholesterol, 26 grams carbohydrates, 34 grams protein, 228 milligrams sodium, 3 grams dietary fiber.

Sassy Salsas A Slimming Choice

Next to ketchup, salsa is the all-American condiment of choice.

OK, so that's not exactly where President Ronald Reagan imagined the condiment wars would lead when he lobbied to get ketchup classified as a vegetable in the federal school lunch program. But from a strictly nutritional point of view, salsa comes a heck of a lot closer to qualifying as a vegetable.

Whether a traditional tomato-based version or an exotic, fruit-based rendition, a sassy salsa can add flavor, color and texture to any dish. It's a clever way to sneak more fruits and vegetables into the diet, upping potassium intake and lowering sodium intake. It's also a slimming choice, compared to cream-based sauces and condiments that quickly add fat and calories.

More and more Americans are in search of flavors to perk up the palate. A recent report in *The Gourmet Retailer* tracked consumer growth in both Caribbean and Jamaican flavored condiments. *The Star's* recipe for Caribbean Pork With Roasted Corn Salsa pairs tender, buttery pork tenderloin marinated in pineapple juice with a light and lively salsa mixture of pineapple, cucumber, red pepper and roasted corn.

Making your own uncooked salsa is not only simple (start chopping) and economical (no need to shell out up to $4 or $5 for a gourmet version), it's also the best way to control your sodium intake. Adults should consume less than 2,300 milligrams of salt a day. Figure that's just a teaspoon a day. Compared to ketchup, store-bought salsas contain about two thirds less sodium but making your own means never having to pick up the salt shaker, a smart move for anyone who suffers from hypertension.

Caribbean Pork Tenderloin With Roasted Corn Salsa

Makes 6 servings

1 cup frozen whole kernel corn
2 (3/4-pound each) pork tenderloins
1 (8-ounce) can crushed pineapple in juice, drained, reserving juice
1 tablespoon olive oil
1/2 teaspoon garlic powder
1/4 teaspoon ground nutmeg
1/4 teaspoon pepper
1/8 teaspoon salt
1/4 cup chopped cucumber
1/2 cup chopped red pepper
2 green onions, chopped
2 tablespoons minced fresh cilantro
2 to 3 drops hot pepper sauce

Preheat oven to 425 degrees. Spray a baking sheet with nonstick vegetable cooking spray. Spread corn in a single layer on baking sheet and spray lightly with nonstick vegetable cooking spray. Bake 15 to 20 minutes or until corn is golden.

Place pork tenderloins on rack of roasting pan. Measure out 2 tablespoons of pineapple juice and reserve it for salsa; combine remaining juice and olive oil. Brush part of juice/oil mixture over pork. Combine garlic powder, nutmeg, pepper and salt and sprinkle over meat. Roast, uncovered, 30 to 35 minutes, until meat thermometer registers 160 degrees for medium doneness. Brush with remaining juice and oil mixture midway through roasting time.

Stir together roasted corn, crushed pineapple, 2 tablespoons reserved juice, cucumber, red pepper, green onions, cilantro and hot pepper sauce. Slice meat and serve with roasted corn salsa.

Per serving: 211 calories (27 percent from fat), 6 grams total fat (2 grams saturated), 74 milligrams cholesterol, 13 grams carbohydrates, 25 grams protein, 106 milligrams sodium, 1 gram dietary fiber.

Shopping Tip: If pineapple or corn is in season, feel free to substitute fresh for canned or frozen products.

Be Open To Sesame

Photo by David Eulitt • THE KANSAS CITY STAR

Look for sesame seeds in the American diet and you're most likely to find them as an edible decoration sprinkled on a hotdog or hamburger bun. But the tiny ivory colored seed may actually be one of the oldest condiments and one of the most nutritious seeds known to man.

A native of Asia, the nutty, slightly sweet seeds were initially brought to the United States by African slaves who called them "benne." Once grown in the South Carolina and Georgia Low Country, the seed eventually became a popular ingredient in Southern cooking.

An herb chart in *The New Food Lover's Companion* (Barron) by Sharon Tyler Herbst also pairs sesame seeds with pork.

Sesame seeds are high in heart-healthy monounsaturated fats, minerals such as copper, manganese and calcium, as well as a host of disease-fighting phytonutrients.

They contain sesaminol compounds, the precursors to lignans, phytoestrograns that are under study for their possible anti-cancer and cardioprotective powers. They also contain zinc, a mineral that ensures bone health and improves the immune system and reproductive health.

The Star's recipe for Tangy Sesame-Coated Pork Chops is a tasty way to get more sesame into your diet. Versatile and economical, lean pork is rich in B vitamins, niacin, phosphorous and potassium.

Tangy Sesame-Coated Pork Chops

Makes 4 servings

4 (6-ounce) lean center-cut loin pork chops,
    approximately 1/2-inch thick
4 tablespoons Dijon mustard
1/3 cup dry bread crumbs
1/3 cup grated Parmesan cheese
2 tablespoons sesame seeds
2 teaspoons dried parsley
    or 2 tablespoons minced fresh parsley
1/2 teaspoon garlic powder

Trim away excess fat from pork chops. Spread 1 tablespoon mustard on sides of each pork chop. Combine remaining ingredients in shallow bowl. Coat pork chops and place in a 9-by-13-inch baking dish that has been coated with nonstick vegetable cooking spray. Bake at 375 degrees 45 minutes or until pork chops are tender.

Per serving: 297 calories (39 percent from fat), 13 grams total fat (4 grams saturated), 82 milligrams cholesterol, 9 grams carbohydrates, 36 grams protein, 454 milligrams sodium, 1 gram dietary fiber.

PUMP IT UP: Make your own bread crumbs using whole-wheat bread instead of white.

Storage Tip: Sesame seeds can be stored in an airtight container in a cool, dry place for up to 3 months or refrigerated for up to 6 months to avoid rancidity.

Fall's Flavors Full Of Nutrition

The abundance of food shipped in from all corners of the globe to American supermarkets can make it difficult to learn how to eat with the seasons.

Consumers can eat ears of sweet corn in May or bundles of asparagus in October. But a lack of seasonal awareness affects not only the freshness and flavor of the foods we put into our shopping carts but also their nutritional value.

That philosophy is distilled in Alice Waters' *The Chez Panisse Menu Cookbook* (Random House).

"If you feed your appetite with second-best foodstuffs for most of the year, you will miss the joyous experience of savoring the tomato during its peak season," the influential Berkeley, Calif.-based chef/owner wrote in her 1982 cookbook.

Waters' insistence on eating seasonally has influenced a generation of chefs and food editors across the country.

The Star's recipe for Apple Glazed Pork Chops pairs two classic fall ingredients. Available year-round, apples are harvested from September to November, and pork is in peak supply between October and February.

Apples are a nutritional powerhouse. Not only are they a good source of vitamins A and C, they also contain flavonoids, a powerful antioxidant compound that has been shown to fend off cardiovascular disease, lung disease, diabetes and cancer.

Although not typically thought of as a health food, today's pork cuts are much leaner than a century ago and contain one-half to one-fifth of the fat they did just 25 years ago, according to Harold McGee, a food scientist and author of *On Food and Cooking: The Science and Lore of the Kitchen* (Scribner).

Apple Glazed Pork Chops

Makes 4 servings

2 teaspoons vegetable oil
1 teaspoon dried thyme leaves
1/2 teaspoon ground nutmeg
1/4 teaspoon salt
1/4 teaspoon pepper
1 pound boneless center-cut pork chops
1 small sweet yellow onion
1 tart red apple, such as Jonathan or Rome,
　　cored and thinly sliced
1 tart green apple, such as Granny Smith,
　　cored and thinly sliced
3/4 cup apple juice
2 tablespoons balsamic vinegar

Heat oil in large nonstick skillet over medium-high heat. Combine thyme, nutmeg, salt and pepper and sprinkle evenly over both sides of chops. Cut onion into 16 to 20 nearly paper-thin wedges. Cook pork chops and onions in oil until chops are well browned on both sides, 7 to 9 minutes.

Add apples and apple juice to skillet. Reduce heat, cover and simmer 25 minutes or until pork and apples are tender. Remove chops to warm serving platter. With a slotted spoon, lift apples and onions from skillet, leaving drippings, and arrange around pork. Increase heat to medium-high. Cook, uncovered, until juices have reduced to about half of original volume, 5 to 8 minutes. Stir in balsamic vinegar and cook, uncovered, 1 minute. Spoon sauce over pork, apples and onions.

Per serving: 278 calories (30 percent from fat), 9 grams total fat (3 grams saturated), 67 milligrams cholesterol, 27 grams carbohydrates, 22 grams protein, 189 milligrams sodium, 4 grams dietary fiber.

COOKING TIP: For a thicker sauce, reduce the apple juice mixture for several minutes over low heat.

Shopping Tip: For the freshest apples and juice, look for locally grown offerings, often found in the produce department.

Island Flavor In Your Backyard

Photo by Tammy Ljungblad • THE KANSAS CITY STAR

An exotic combination of grilled meat, fruit and vegetables makes a meal.

Feel like you're suddenly stranded on a deserted patch of burnt grass while family, friends, neighbors and co-workers are lounging in a vacation hammock by the sea?

Don't get mad. Get even. Plan your own mini luau.

The highlight of the traditional Hawaiian feast is a roast pig, something few home cooks would ever have the time or inclination to prepare.

By downsizing the concept, you can capture those same exotic flavors but skip the back-breaking labor of digging a pit. Just thread a skewer with lean pork tenderloin in a Polynesian-inspired marinade with fresh pineapple.

It's long been understood that pineapple contains vitamin C, which helps keep the immune system functioning properly. In recent years pineapple continues to receive the thumbs-up. The tropical fruit contains the enzyme called bromelain, an anti-inflammatory that research shows may relieve the swelling of arthritis as well as reduce blood clots, lowering the risk for stroke or heart attack.

The Star's recipe for Pork And Pineapple Kebabs also has chunks of fruits and vegetables that are as nutritious as they are colorful on the plate: red onion (quercetin), red pepper (beta carotene), sweet potato (beta carotene, lutein and zeaxanthin) and papaya (vitamin C, vitamin E and beta carotene).

SHOPPING TIPS: When buying a fresh pineapple, choose one that is fragrant. It also should be heavy for its size. Avoid brown spots and be sure the leaves are green.

Pre-cut pineapple chunks are available on the salad bar at most supermarkets.

Pork And
Pineapple Kebabs

Makes 6 servings

1 pound pork tenderloin, cut into 1-inch cubes
1/4 cup pineapple juice
2 tablespoons reduced-sodium soy sauce
2 tablespoons lime juice
2 tablespoons honey
1 tablespoon grated fresh ginger
2 cloves garlic, minced
1 jalapeño pepper, seeded and minced
1 teaspoon vegetable oil
1 sweet potato, peeled and
    cut into 1-inch cubes
1/2 fresh pineapple, cut into 1 1/2-inch cubes
    (about 1 1/4 cups)
1/2 red onion, cut into wedges
    about 3/4-inch thick
1 papaya, peeled, seeded and sliced into strips
    about 1 1/2-inches wide
1/2 large red pepper, seeded and cut into
    1 1/2-inch pieces

Cooking Tip: Papaya is difficult to grill. To avoid having pieces fall through the grate, skewer twice, or leave it off the skewer and use as a garnish.

Place pork cubes in zipper-top plastic bag. Combine pineapple juice, soy sauce, lime juice, honey, ginger, garlic and jalapeño pepper; stir to combine. Pour 3 tablespoons juice mixture over pork; seal bag and refrigerate several hours or overnight. Cover and refrigerate remaining juice mixture.

Preheat grill to medium-high or allow coals to burn down to white ash. Drain meat and discard marinade. Stir oil into reserved juice mixture. Place sweet potato cubes in small glass or microwave-safe bowl. Add 2 teaspoons water. Cover and microwave on high 2 to 2 1/2 minutes or until crisp-tender. Uncover and allow to cool slightly. Alternately thread pork cubes, sweet potato cubes, pineapple, red onion wedges, papaya pieces and red pepper onto 6 skewers. Place kebabs in shallow baking dish or tray. Brush generously with juice mixture. Grill 15 to 18 minutes or until pork is just slightly pink when cut, for medium doneness, turning so they brown evenly and brushing with remaining juice mixture midway through cooking.

Per serving: 199 calories (16 percent from fat), 4 grams total fat (1 gram saturated), 49 milligrams cholesterol, 25 grams carbohydrates, 18 grams protein, 244 milligrams sodium, 3 grams dietary fiber.

Apricots In An Altered State

No doubt you've heard fresh is best.

But in the case of an apricot, the dried fruit contains an advantage over fresh.

Apricots are an excellent source of vitamin A, a nutrient essential to good vision. But fresh or dried apricots that have been cooked contain even more beta carotene, an antioxidant the body converts to vitamin A. Cooking the apricot also releases lycopene, an antioxidant, and pectin, a soluble fiber that lowers LDL cholesterol, according to Fight Back With Food by Reader's Digest.

Nutrition experts explain this phenomenon with a fancy word: bioavailability.

It's a relatively simple concept: The form in which a food is consumed—fresh, dried or cooked—may affect the percentage of the nutrient absorbed by the body. What it is eaten with can also play a role.

The Star's recipe for Apricot Pork Chops pairs a lean chop with dried apricots, both foods high in iron. Iron is more easily absorbed when paired with foods that are high in vitamin C. By cooking the apricots in orange juice, you're not only creating a delicious sauce, but you're also making the iron more available.

But the real benefit?

The foods taste great together.

STORAGE TIP: Wrapped in a plastic bag, dried fruit can be kept at room temperature for up to a year. If the apricots become too dry, the orange juice in this recipe will help to rehydrate them.

Photo by Tammy Ljungblad • THE KANSAS CITY STAR

Apricot Pork Chops

Makes 4 servings

1/2 cup chopped dried apricots
1/2 cup orange juice
1/4 cup apricot preserves
2 teaspoons brown sugar
1/2 teaspoon curry powder
2 teaspoons olive oil
4 small boneless loin pork chops, each 1/2 to 3/4 inch
    thick (about 1 pound total)
Salt and pepper to taste
2 green onions, chopped

Place apricots in a deep bowl. Pour orange juice over apricots. Add preserves, brown sugar and curry powder and stir gently. Set aside.

Heat a large skillet over medium-high heat. Add oil. Cook chops about 3 minutes on each side or until browned. Season lightly with salt and pepper.

Reduce heat to low. Add apricot and juice mixture. Cover and simmer about 5 minutes or until pork chops reach 160 degrees on meat thermometer.

Remove from heat and sprinkle with green onions.

Per serving: 293 calories (22 percent from fat), 7 grams total fat (2 grams saturated), 51 milligrams cholesterol, 37 grams carbohydrates, 22 grams protein, 55 milligrams sodium, 3 grams dietary fiber.

COOKING TIP: To keep dried fruit from sticking to your knife when chopping, spray the blade with a thin coating of vegetable cooking spray.

Shopping Tip: Dried fruit is often treated with sulfur dioxide, which prevents it from turning brown. If you are sensitive to sulfites, look for sulfite-free apricots in health-food stores.

Photo by Tammy Ljungblad • THE KANSAS CITY STAR

The Skinny On Slim Cuts Of Pork

Say the word "lean" and chances are you'll think of beef, chicken or fish, but rarely pork.

If you know how to choose the right cut, there's no reason to steer clear of "the other white meat." Yet only 24 percent of Americans know pork is a lean source of protein, according to a recent consumer survey conducted for the National Pork Board.

Six cuts qualify as "slim," including the pork tenderloin featured in *The Star's* Grilled Pork Tenderloin And Red Pepper Coulis.

Other cuts to look for: pork boneless top loin chop, pork top loin roast (boneless), pork center loin chop, pork center rib chop and pork sirloin roasts (bone-in).

Enjoy lean pork and earthy portabellas topped with an antioxidant-rich red pepper coulis—that's a fancy name you've probably seen on high-end restaurant menus that means a thick puree or sauce.

Grilled Pork Tenderloin With Red Pepper Coulis

Makes 6 servings

For the coulis:
1 (12-ounce) jar roasted red peppers,
    rinsed and drained
2 tablespoons tomato paste
1 tablespoon unsalted butter
1 cup finely chopped sweet onion
3 cloves garlic, minced
1/2 cup red wine
Freshly ground pepper to taste
1 cup reduced-sodium beef broth
1 tablespoon cornstarch

For the pork:
2 tablespoons olive oil
2 cloves garlic, minced
1/4 teaspoon salt
1/2 teaspoon pepper
1 pork tenderloin, about 1 pound
2 tablespoons red wine
2 whole portabella mushrooms, sliced about 3/4-inch thick
18 to 24 leafy salad greens, rinsed and patted dry

Make-Ahead Tip: Red pepper coulis is great over any grilled meat, chicken or fish. It may be frozen, if desired.

For the coulis: Place red peppers in work bowl of food processor; process until smooth. Add tomato paste and process to combine. Melt butter in saucepan over medium heat. Add onion and garlic and cook, stirring frequently, until onion is tender. Stir in pepper puree, wine and pepper. Stir in broth and cornstarch until completely blended; pour broth mixture into pepper mixture. Cook, uncovered, over medium-low heat 20 to 25 minutes, stirring occasionally.

For the pork: Combine olive oil, garlic, salt and pepper. Measure 1 tablespoon oil mixture and rub over pork, covering evenly. Stir wine into remaining oil mixture. Place mushrooms in zip-top plastic bag. Pour wine-oil mixture over all; seal and shake gently to coat. Preheat grill. Grill pork over direct heat, turning frequently to cook evenly, 15 to 20 minutes or until meat thermometer registers 160 degrees. Cover and allow to stand 5 to 10 minutes; cut into 1-inch slices. Drain mushrooms; grill over direct heat 3 to 4 minutes per side. Arrange greens and slices of mushroom and pork on each plate. Drizzle 3 to 4 tablespoons coulis over each serving.

Per serving (pork and coulis): 185 calories (39 percent from fat), 8 grams total fat (2 grams saturated), 52 milligrams cholesterol, 8 grams carbohydrates, 18 grams protein, 199 milligrams sodium, 2 grams fiber.

Lamb Tickles The Tastebuds

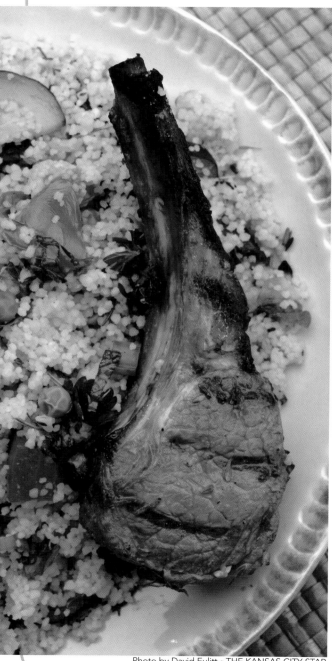

Photo by David Eulitt • THE KANSAS CITY STAR

If sun-dried tomatoes, Kalamata olives or couscous (KOOS-kooz) are staples of your pantry, chances are you first ate them in a restaurant. So let's give credit where credit is due.

Top-flight restaurant chefs are taste innovators, and they're typically a few steps ahead of the mainstream food trends. Of course, it's hard to predict what will tickle our tastebuds. Goat cheese is surely a food for the masses, but lamb, which has long been a restaurant menu favorite, has never managed to become a staple of the American dinner table.

In a never-ending quest for portion control, lamb ribs—sometimes whimsically referred to by chefs as "lamb popsicles"—are a fun way to feel like you're indulging without actually going completely off the deep end. Ah, pick them up with your fingers and gnaw. It satisfies a primal urge, but without the heavily marbled, big-steak guilt.

Lamb is a lean protein source with vitamin B12, iron, niacin and zinc. A 3-ounce serving, about the size of a deck of cards, offers nearly half of the protein the average person needs in a day.

The Star's Grilled Lamb Chops With Vegetable Couscous Pilaf is a well-rounded meal for traditionalists providing a meat, starch and vegetable, yet the Middle Eastern flavor accent is a nice departure for anyone craving more excitement from their meals.

Couscous—another food that was almost unheard of a decade ago—is a wonderful accompaniment for lamb. Couscous is granular, quick-cooking semolina that can be used as you would rice, potatoes or pasta. Originally a staple of North African cuisine, it is readily available in the ethnic foods aisle of most large supermarkets.

Swordfish With Tomato Basil Caper Sauce

Makes 4 to 6 servings

2 tablespoons olive oil
1 cup chopped sweet onion
2 cloves garlic, minced
1 (28-ounce) can plum tomatoes, partly drained
1/4 cup dry white wine
1/2 cup chopped fresh basil
2 tablespoons capers, drained
2 swordfish fillets (about 1 to 1 1/2 pounds)
Salt and pepper to taste
Fresh basil leaves for garnish, optional

Heat oil in saucepan over medium heat. Add onions, reduce heat to low and cook 10 minutes. Add garlic and cook 30 seconds. Add the tomatoes, using a spoon to break into pieces. Simmer 15 minutes; add wine and cook 10 minutes more to reduce liquid. Stir basil and capers into tomato mixture and cook 1 minute.

Preheat grill and allow to burn down to white coals. Spray fish with nonstick vegetable cooking spray and sprinkle lightly with salt and generously with pepper. Grill over high heat 5 minutes on each side or until the center is cooked through. Spoon tomato sauce on plate and place fish on top. Garnish with fresh basil.

Per serving, based on 4: 250 calories (44 percent from fat), 12 grams total fat (2 grams saturated), 44 milligrams cholesterol, 10 grams carbohydrates, 24 grams protein, 153 milligrams sodium, 2 grams dietary fiber.

COOKING TIP: Swordfish can easily dry out from overcooking. Finished steaks should be well-browned, while the interior should remain moist.

Shopping Tip: Other fish with higher levels of methylmercury include king mackerel, shark, tilefish and tuna (fresh and frozen). In general, smaller fish have less mercury (including canned tuna). If you're in an at-risk group or you're not comfortable choosing swordfish for this recipe, substitute Pacific or Alaskan halibut instead.

Photo by Tammy Ljungblad • THE KANSAS CITY STAR

A Saucy Asian Translation

Like the armchair traveler who is content to read about daring adventures, prepared Asian stir-fry sauces hold out the promise of new and exotic tastes—without the dangers of deciphering ingredient labels in a foreign language.

But sadly, when it comes to flavor, something is usually lost in translation.

Unlike classical French sauces and reductions, Asian sauces are relatively simple to pull together. Whisk together a few uncomplicated ingredients and skip the MSG (monosodium glutamate, an allergy trigger for some people) and the preservatives. Making your own also allows you to control the amount of sodium and sugar.

The Star's Fish And Vegetables In Thai Sauce combines rice vinegar, honey, garlic, pepper flakes and vegetable oil to create a sauce so fragrant I was getting requests for a copy of the recipe from colleagues based on the smell alone. Not surprisingly, scientists estimate 80 percent of a food's flavor is in its aroma.

The fish and vegetables in this dish are prepared using two low-fat cooking techniques: The fish is broiled while the vegetables are stir-fried. Both techniques keep added fats to a minimum.

Fish And Vegetables
In Thai Sauce

Makes 4 servings

Serving Tip: This sauce would also go well with chicken and seafood.

2 firm-textured fish fillets, 8 to 9 ounces each
1/2 cup rice vinegar
1/4 cup honey
4 cloves garlic, minced
1/4 teaspoon crushed red pepper flakes
2 teaspoons vegetable oil
1 red pepper, cut into strips
   about 1/4-inch wide
1 small zucchini, cut into strips
   about 2-by 1/4-inches
1 cup sliced mushrooms
2 tablespoons minced cilantro, optional

Place fish in zip-top plastic food bag. Combine vinegar, honey, garlic and red pepper flakes; spoon 3 tablespoons vinegar mixture over fish. Seal bag, turn to coat well and allow to marinate 15 minutes. Reserve remaining vinegar mixture.

Spray broiler pan with nonstick vegetable cooking spray. Drain fish and place on broiler pan. Broil 5 minutes, turn and broil about 3 minutes or just until fish is done and flakes easily.

Meanwhile, heat oil in large skillet over medium-high heat. Add vegetables and stir-fry 2 minutes. Pour reserved vinegar mixture over vegetables and heat to boil. Boil 30 seconds, stirring constantly.

Arrange vegetables and sauce on serving plate. Top with fish, then spoon sauce over top of fish. Sprinkle with cilantro, if desired.

Per serving: 208 calories (14 percent from fat), 3 grams total fat (trace saturated fat), 49 milligrams cholesterol, 25 grams carbohydrates, 22 grams protein, 68 milligrams sodium, 2 grams dietary fiber.

COOKING TIP: We tested this with salmon, grouper and halibut. Do not over-marinate the fish or it will become mushy.

No Need To Fear Tilapia

Tilapia is:
  a.) a Siberian lap dog
  b.) a tasty pudding
  c.) a mild-tasting white fish
  d.) none of the above

This quiz appeared on a T-shirt worn by a member of the Tilapia Marketing Institute in the late '90s. A few years later the National Fisheries Institute reported the mild-tasting white fish had inched onto the Top 10 seafood list. But even with clever marketing ploys, Midwestern consumers sometimes still feel like fish out of water.

Turns out, tilapia is for the timid.

A freshwater fish, tilapia stays fresh longer than saltwater fish varieties during shipping. Tilapia's mild, firm-textured flesh with few bones pairs well with a host of flavors and is adaptable to a variety of cooking methods, including baking, broiling, grilling, poaching, braising and steaming.

Tilapia can be substituted in recipes that call for sole, snapper, flounder, cod, sea bass and orange roughly. An excellent source of protein minus the saturated fats, The Star's Mediterranean Fish Fillets are a heart healthy choice: a 4-ounce tilapia fillet contains about 90 milligrams of omega-3 fatty acid.

Tilapia is sometimes referred to as "St. Peter's" fish because legend says it is the fish from biblical times. More recently tilapia was flown on the shuttle to see whether they could thrive in space station fish farms.

As one of the most important food fishes in the world, tilapia is bred in fresh-water ponds on every continent around the world except Antarctica. In the United States, tilapia production is concentrated in Texas, Arizona and Florida.

Photo by Jim Barcus • THE KANSAS CITY STAR

Mediterranean Fish Fillets

Makes 6 servings

1 teaspoon olive oil
1/2 cup chopped onion
1/4 cup chopped green pepper
1 cup sliced mushrooms
2 cloves garlic, minced
3 Roma tomatoes, seeded and chopped
1 teaspoon dried basil leaves
1 teaspoon dried oregano leaves
1/4 teaspoon sugar
1/8 teaspoon crushed red pepper flakes
Dash of salt
1/4 cup white wine
1 1/2 pound tilapia fish fillets
2 tablespoons grated Parmesan cheese

Heat oil in saucepan over medium-high heat. Add onion and green pepper and cook, stirring frequently, until tender. Add mushrooms and garlic and cook 2 minutes. Stir in tomatoes, basil, oregano, sugar, red pepper flakes, salt and wine; simmer 5 to 10 minutes.

Preheat oven to 425 degrees. Spray a 9-by-13-inch baking dish with nonstick vegetable cooking spray. Arrange fish fillets in a single layer in pan. Top with tomato sauce. Bake, uncovered, 10 minutes or until fish is opaque and flakes easily with a fork. Sprinkle with grated Parmesan.

Per serving: 150 calories (19 percent from fat), 3 grams total fat (1 gram saturated), 43 milligrams cholesterol, 4 grams carbohydrates, 25 grams protein, 150 milligrams sodium, 1 gram dietary fiber.

Shopping Tip: Frozen tilapia can last for up to six months, according to aboutseafood.com, a Web site sponsored by the National Fisheries Institute. Never refreeze fish. Thaw in the refrigerator; discard any fish that is mushy when thawed.

A Savory Soaking Before Grilling

Photo by Tammy Ljungblad • THE KANSAS CITY STAR

Chefs use marinades to make foods tender and infuse them with flavor.

But scientists have discovered marinades also act as a barrier to potentially carcinogenic substances that are created when meat and fish are cooked over flames. Using a marinade before grilling reduces HCA (heterocyclic amines) by 92 percent to 99 percent, according to American Institute for Cancer Research (aicr.org).

The Star's Grilled Salmon Salad features an Asian-inspired soy marinade that gives the heart-healthy salmon a moist, delicious flavor. The fish is paired with a farmers market complement of fresh vegetables, including pea pods, asparagus and tomatoes. A final sprinkling of sesame seeds supplies loads of flavor and phytonutrients.

COOKING TIPS: The salmon for this recipe can be fresh or thawed. Frozen salmon may be smaller, and if so, cook 4 4-ounce fillets in similar fashion, reducing cooking time if necessary. Be sure not to overcook the fish.

Snap ends from asparagus and, if desired, remove scales with a vegetable peeler.

Trim ends from pea pods and remove strings before cooking.

Grilled Salmon Salad

Makes 4 servings

2 salmon fillets, about 8 ounces each
8 asparagus spears
1/3 cup freshly squeezed lime juice
2 tablespoons brown sugar
1 tablespoon sesame oil
2 tablespoons reduced-sodium soy sauce
2 cloves garlic, minced
2 teaspoons grated fresh ginger
1 tablespoon seasoned rice vinegar
1 1/2 cups fresh snow pea pods, trimmed
6 cups torn salad greens
1 tablespoon sesame seeds, toasted
2 Roma tomatoes, sliced

To Toast Seeds: Bake sesame seeds at 350 degrees 4 to 5 minutes or until just golden. Watch closely so they don't burn.

Place salmon fillets in zip-top plastic food bag. Trim asparagus spears and place in another bag. Combine lime juice, brown sugar, sesame oil, soy sauce, garlic and ginger; stir well to combine. Drizzle 2 tablespoons lime juice mixture over salmon; seal bag. Drizzle 1 tablespoon lime juice mixture over asparagus; seal bag. Turn bags to coat evenly, then refrigerate about 30 minutes. Stir vinegar into remaining lime juice mixture; cover and refrigerate.

Preheat grill or allow coals to burn down to white ash. Spray grate with nonstick vegetable cooking spray or lightly oil it.

Remove salmon from bag; drain and discard marinade. Grill salmon 4 to 5 minutes per side, or until fish flakes easily with a fork.

Remove asparagus from bag; drain and discard marinade. Grill asparagus until just fork tender, 5 to 7 minutes, turning to cook evenly.

Meanwhile, heat a small amount of water to a boil in a covered saucepan. Once water boils, add pea pods, cover and cook about 2 minutes or until hot but still crisp. Drain pea pods and plunge into ice water.

Arrange salad greens on 4 individual plates. Top each salad with 1/2 of a hot, cooked salmon fillet. (If salmon fillets have skin, remove before serving.) Sprinkle sesame seeds evenly over salmon. Arrange asparagus spears, pea pods and sliced tomatoes on each salad. Drizzle with reserved lime juice mixture.

Per serving: 257 calories (30 percent from fat), 9 grams total fat (1 gram saturated), 59 milligrams cholesterol, 19 grams carbohydrates, 28 grams protein, 357 milligrams sodium, 5 grams dietary fiber.

Ancient Pomegranate Reborn

From the Charbizzle Pomegrizzle cocktail at JP Wine Bar in downtown Kansas City to the Pomegranate Frappuccino at Starbuck's, the ancient fruit is turning into a thoroughly modern superstar.

In fact, straight-up pomegranate juice is muscling its way to the front of the refrigerated juice case in the produce section of major supermarkets.

The ruby-red juice of the pomegranate has been an indispensable part of the Persian pantry since biblical times. But its emerging superfood status has given the fruit new cachet. *The Star's* Grilled Shrimp With Gingered Pomegranate Sauce gives a sweet/tart twist to this modern shrimp kebab dish.

Rich in potassium and a good source of vitamins B6 and C, pomegranate juice has three times more

COOKING TIP: Pomegranate juice is sometimes used as a dye. Keep in mind it can stain whatever it touches.

antioxidant power than green tea or red wine. Research indicates these compounds help lower blood pressure and bad cholesterol.

A study published in *Clinical Cancer Research*, a peer-reviewed journal of the American Association of Cancer Research, found that pomegranate juice appears to help keep PSA levels stable in men with prostate cancer.

Conducted by UCLA researchers—and funded by Pom Wonderful, a leading brand of pomegranate juice —it included 50 men who drank an 8-ounce glass of pomegranate juice daily. After three years, the men's PSA (prostate-specific antigen), a biomarker for cancer, remained stable nearly four times longer.

"I think the research is definitely getting out there, but I think marketing is putting it into the mainstream," says Abby Heidari, a registered dietitian at the Hy-Vee supermarket in Leawood.

Grilled Shrimp With Gingered Pomegranate Sauce

Makes 4 servings

1 pound large shrimp in the shell, uncooked, deveined, tails on
1/2 teaspoon garlic powder
1/4 teaspoon cayenne pepper
Salt and pepper to taste
1 tablespoon plus 1 teaspoon olive oil, divided
2 cloves garlic, minced
2 green onions, finely chopped, divided
1 teaspoon grated fresh ginger
2/3 cup pomegranate juice
3 tablespoons chopped parsley
1 tablespoon butter

Place shrimp in bowl. Sprinkle with garlic powder, cayenne pepper, salt and pepper; toss to coat. Drizzle with 1 tablespoon olive oil; toss to coat shrimp.

Preheat grill or allow coals to burn down to white ash. Skewer shrimp on kebab skewers for easy grilling. Place shrimp on grill and cook 6 minutes, turning once. (The shrimp are cooked when they are firm and white with bright pink shells.) Allow to cool slightly, then remove shells.

Heat remaining 1 teaspoon olive oil in nonstick medium skillet over medium-high heat. Add garlic and half of green onions. Cook until garlic is tender but not brown. Add ginger and juice. Simmer 5 minutes until juice is reduced; gently stir in parsley. Gently stir in butter until melted.

To serve, drizzle sauce over shrimp and garnish with remaining green onions.

Per serving: 206 calories (37 percent from fat), 8 grams total fat (3 grams saturated), 180 milligrams cholesterol, 8 grams carbohydrates, 24 grams protein, 205 milligrams sodium, trace dietary fiber.

Shopping Tip: Pomegranate juice is not inexpensive. To get the most bang for your buck, look for 100-percent pomegranate juice with no added sugar.

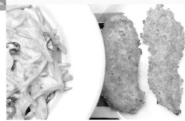

Kids
Meals

4

Breakfast On A Stick

Photo by Tammy Ljungblad • THE KANSAS CITY STAR

Look, Ma! No bowl.

In the hustle and bustle that starts the day, breakfast is a meal that typically gets short shrift—especially if you're not a cereal eater. But there's no reason a bowl and spoon are required gear for the morning munch. The Star's Strawberry Smoothie Breakfast Pops are a clever way to get kids off to a good start.

A yogurt-based fruit smoothie has long been a healthful way to start the day. Ancient Greeks and Romans are believed to have eaten yogurt, according to Prevention Magazine's Nutrition Advisor (Rodale Press). Yogurt has continued to be a staple food for the people of the Middle East and Eastern Europe for thousands of years.

No time to sit down at the table and engage in this delicious ancient ritual?

The addition of a Popsicle stick makes it the perfect American-style grab-and-go breakfast. It's really no surprise that the more convenient—and cool—the food, the less likely teenagers are to snooze through breakfast.

Numerous studies have shown that forgetting to "break" the "fast" can lead to poor memory, a lack of concentration and a generally crabby mood. Skipping breakfast means teens often do not make up that lack of calcium later in the day, a crucial deficiency during rapid bone-building years that may lead to osteoporosis later in life.

One cup of yogurt contains more calcium than a glass of milk. Look for yogurt that contains at least 35 percent to 40 percent of the recommended daily calcium.

Yogurt is also an excellent source of protein and includes magnesium and potassium, important nutrients that when consumed with calcium can help regulate blood pressure. Add strawberries and bananas, a satisfying flavor combination as well as a source of vitamins and fiber.

For anyone who is lactose-intolerant, yogurt is often more easily digested than milk.

Strawberry Smoothie Yogurt Breakfast Pops

Makes 8 to 9 servings

1 to 2 bananas
1 tablespoon lemon juice
2 (6-ounce) cartons low-fat strawberry yogurt
1 (16-ounce) package frozen
    whole strawberries, partially thawed,
    with juice
2 teaspoons confectioners' sugar
1/4 cup fat-free skim milk

Storage Tip: For longer storage, place several frozen cups in large zip-top plastic food bags.

Place bananas and lemon juice in blender; blend until smooth. Add remaining ingredients and blend until smooth. Pour mixture into 5-ounce paper drinking cups. Arrange filled cups on tray. Stand a wooden Popsicle stick upright in each cup. Freeze overnight.

Per serving, based on 8: 81 calories (7 percent from fat), 1 gram total fat (trace saturated fat), 2 milligrams cholesterol, 18 grams carbohydrates, 2 grams protein, 28 milligrams sodium, 2 grams dietary fiber.

PUMP IT UP: This recipe is adjustable to just about any yogurt flavor and fruit combination. Prefer vanilla yogurt with blueberries or peach yogurt with sliced peaches? Go for it. The calorie count will vary only slightly.

Photo by Tammy Ljungblad • THE KANSAS CITY STAR

Downsizing Ups The Nutrition

Sure, lots of good things come in small packages, just usually not muffins.

In theory, a muffin should automatically promote portion control. But in recent years, the muffin has mushroomed into something approaching monstrous.

C'mon, even when you do grab a mini muffin, you usually eat more than one. Right?

The average commercially sold muffin is now several sizes too big for its crinkled paper cup and is loaded with excess goodies that add fat and calories to the American diet.

The Star's Carrot Raisin Muffins knock things back down to a realistic portion size. Figure a muffin should measure about the size of a tennis ball.

Studies have shown that cutting portions, rather than cutting out the foods you love, can help maintain a desirable weight.

At the same time we were right-sizing our muffin, we also found ways to pump up its nutritional profile.

To reduce the amount of fat, use applesauce, egg whites and fat-free milk.

Stir in whole-grain oats and carrots to pump up the fiber content.

Replace some of the sugar with raisins, a sweet, low-fat, high-energy dried fruit containing plenty of phytonutrients as well as boron, a trace mineral that promotes bone health. In addition to adding fiber and sweetness, the carrots also offer impressive amounts of beta-carotene, a precursor for vitamin A.

Carrot Raisin Muffins

Makes 12 muffins

2 cups all-purpose flour
1 cup rolled oats
2/3 cup sugar
1 tablespoon baking powder
1/2 teaspoon ground cinnamon
1/2 teaspoon ground nutmeg
1/4 teaspoon salt
2/3 cup fat-free skim milk
3 tablespoons vegetable oil
2 egg whites
1/4 cup unsweetened applesauce
1/3 cup golden raisins
1 1/4 cups shredded carrot

Preheat oven to 400 degrees. Line 12 muffin cups with baking papers. Lightly spray paper cups with nonstick vegetable cooking spray. Combine flour, oats, sugar, baking powder, cinnamon, nutmeg and salt in a large mixing bowl. Combine milk, oil, egg whites and apple-sauce in a smaller bowl; blend into flour mixture, stirring just until moistened. Stir in raisins and carrots. Spoon batter into prepared muffin pans, filling each about 3/4 full. Bake 16 to 18 minutes or until golden.

Per muffin: 205 calories (18 percent from fat), 4 grams total fat (1 gram saturated), trace cholesterol, 38 grams carbohydrates, 5 grams protein, 188 milligrams sodium, 2 grams dietary fiber.

Cooking Tip: Lower-fat muffins tend to stick to the paper liners more than higher-fat muffins. Spraying the paper cups with nonstick vegetable cooking spray makes it easier to peel off the papers. These muffins taste best served warm.

Whole, Wheat And Blue

Photo by David Eulitt • THE KANSAS CITY STAR

The recent flood of whole-grain products hitting supermarket shelves can leave shoppers feeling like they're playing the game "Where's Waldo?"

Scan the nutrition label and you're likely to find terms like "100 percent wheat," "multigrain" and "stone ground." Sure, they sound good, but they don't actually mean a product contains whole grains.

The USDA's MyPyramid encourages Americans to get enough whole-grain foods into their diets. New recommendations advise at least three servings a day of whole grains, and one of the easiest ways to get more into your diet is to simply add some whole-wheat flour to baked goods.

Unlike conventional all-purpose flour, whole-wheat flour contains wheat germ which makes it higher in fiber. But don't go overboard: Using just whole-wheat flour can produce heavy, leaden baked goods. That's why bakers typically use half whole-wheat flour and half all-purpose flour.

The Star's Whole-Wheat Blueberry Muffins uses egg whites and skim milk to take some of the fat out of these protein- and fiber-rich muffins. While low-calorie blueberries add flavor and keep the muffin moist, they're also high in fiber, potassium and vitamin C. Loaded with antioxidants, blueberries help fight infections, heal wounds and enhance the absorption of iron from other foods.

Whole-Wheat Blueberry Muffins

Makes 12 muffins

1 cup all-purpose flour
1 cup whole-wheat flour
2 cups fresh blueberries,
    or frozen blueberries,
    thawed and well-drained
1 tablespoon baking powder
1/4 teaspoon salt
1/3 cup butter, softened
3/4 cup sugar
3 egg whites
1/2 cup fat-free skim milk
1 teaspoon vanilla extract

Storage Tip: Because it has a higher fat content, store whole-wheat flour in the refrigerator to avoid rancidity.

Preheat oven to 375 degrees. Line muffin tin cups with paper baking cups. Stir together flour and whole-wheat flour. Measure out 1 tablespoon flour mixture and sprinkle over blueberries; toss to coat evenly and set aside. Stir baking powder and salt into flour mixture; set aside.

Beat butter and sugar together until creamy. Beat in egg whites until well-combined. Stir in milk and vanilla. Stir in flour mixture, blending just until softened. Stir in blueberries. Spoon into muffin cups, filling nearly to the top of each cup. Bake 25 minutes or until golden brown.

Per muffin: 198 calories (26 percent from fat), 6 grams total fat (3 grams saturated), 14 milligrams cholesterol, 32 grams carbohydrates, 4 grams protein, 240 milligrams sodium, 2 grams dietary fiber.

Wake Up Your Tastebuds

Photo by David Eulitt • THE KANSAS CITY STAR

G ranola, that back-to-nature mixture of oats, fruits and nuts, was first hip to the natural foods crowd in the '70s. Today it's considered so mainstream even McDonald's sells a yogurt and fruit parfait topped with a modest dusting of granola.

A longtime granola fan, Rebecca Miller considers the whole-grain/fruit/nut mixture "the perfect food," as well as a creative teaching tool to talk about good nutrition.

"You can control exactly what's going in it, from the spices, to the cooking oil or fat, to the different cereals that are fun to play with," says Miller, marketing director for Whole Foods in Overland Park.

Developed by a Swiss nutritionist at the end of the 19th century, granola is an easy way to get the benefit of whole grains which adds B vitamins, fiber and minerals into your diet. The only caveat is that commercial granola brands are often high in oil and added sugar. So if you're not a careful label reader, skip the store-bought versions and make your own instead.

The Star's Blueberry Cashew Granola is a tasty alternative that allows you to control the fat content—in this case a very small amount of heart-healthy canola oil combined with a mixture of honey and molasses for sweetness.

Blueberry Cashew Granola

Makes 10 servings (about 1/2 cup each)

2 1/2 cups old-fashioned rolled oats
2/3 cup unsalted cashew halves
1/2 cup wheat germ
1/3 cup unsalted sunflower seeds
1/3 cup molasses
1/3 cup honey
1 tablespoon canola oil
1 1/2 teaspoons cinnamon
1/2 teaspoon nutmeg
1 cup dried blueberries

Preheat oven to 275 degrees. Line a baking sheet with aluminum foil and spray with nonstick vegetable cooking spray.

Combine the oats, cashews, wheat germ and sunflower seeds in a large bowl. In a separate bowl, combine the molasses, honey, oil, cinnamon and nutmeg. Pour molasses mixture over oat mixture and stir well to combine. Spread evenly in prepared pan.

Bake 30 minutes or until golden, stirring after 15 minutes and frequently after that. Remove from oven and cool completely. Stir blueberries into granola mixture.

Per serving: 317 calories (27 percent from fat), 10 grams total fat (2 grams saturated), no cholesterol, 52 grams carbohydrates, 8 grams protein, 8 milligrams sodium, 6 grams dietary fiber.

PREPARATION TIP: This recipe freezes well, so don't shy away because of the large serving size.

PUMP IT UP: Granola is not just for breakfast anymore. Add a sprinkle of granola to puddings, yogurt, ice cream, a bowl of fresh fruit. Or simply eat it out of hand as a snack.

Shopping Tips: Look for dried blueberries in the produce aisle or the baking aisle with the dried fruits, such as raisins.

Instant oats and old-fashioned rolled oats are not interchangeable. Instant oats have been pre-cooked and dried.

Wake Up To Whole Grains

Photo by Tammy Ljungblad • THE KANSAS CITY STAR

What's better than sliced bread?

Whole-grain breads are nutritionally superior to soft, spongy white breads.

The USDA's MyPyramid recommends Americans eat three or more servings of whole grains a day to reduce the risk of cancers and heart disease. But consumption of whole-grain foods like bread has declined by more than half since 1900.

If you're having trouble working more whole grains into your diet, breakfast is a good place to start. Just watch out for whole-grain breads with junk ingredients. Recently I reached for a loaf of store-baked whole-grain bread and was shocked to discover the second ingredient was high-fructose corn syrup.

Buying a true whole-grain bread can be tricky. Look for 100 percent on the label, whole-wheat flour as the first ingredient, 2 grams of fiber per ounce and the heart disease health claim, writes Marion Nestle, a nationally respected nutrition expert and author of *What to Eat* (North Point Press).

"Anything else is reconstituted white bread with varying amounts of whole grains added," Nestle concludes.

The Star's recipe for Whole-Grain French Toast With Fresh Berries makes a tasty breakfast or brunch entrée. Dip the bread in a mixture of soy milk, orange juice and egg white. Bake until golden-brown. Top each slice with 1/2 cup of fresh seasonal berries for a whopping dose of vitamins, fiber and health-promoting phytonutrients.

Strawberry fruit spread replaces the artificial sweetness of most pancake syrups. A dollop of low-fat yogurt adds a dose of calcium as well as touch of class.

Whole-Grain French Toast With Fresh Berries

Makes 4 servings

1/3 cup plain soy milk
6 tablespoons orange juice, divided
1 egg white
1 teaspoon confectioners' sugar
1/2 teaspoon cinnamon
1/2 teaspoon vanilla
4 thick slices whole-grain bakery-style bread
    (about 1-inch thick)
1/4 cup strawberry fruit spread
2 cups fresh berries (strawberries,
    raspberries and blueberries)
Strawberry flavored low-fat yogurt for garnish

Cooking Tip: Feel free to experiment with vanilla-flavored soy milk.

Preheat oven to 450 degrees. Line a baking sheet with aluminum foil; spray foil with nonstick vegetable cooking spray.

Combine soy milk, 1/4 cup orange juice, egg white, confectioners' sugar, cinnamon and vanilla in a pie plate or deep dish; whisk gently until blended.

Dip each slice of bread into liquid mixture, turning to coat evenly on both sides. Place in single layer on baking sheet.

Bake 8 minutes. Turn and bake second side 5 minutes or until bread is lightly crisp. Meanwhile, whisk together strawberry fruit spread and remaining 2 tablespoons orange juice in a large mixing bowl. Add berries and stir gently to coat evenly.

To serve, top each slice of French toast with about 1/2 cup berry topping and a dollop of yogurt.

Per serving: 137 calories (11 percent from fat), 2 grams total fat (trace saturated fat), no cholesterol, 27 grams carbohydrates, 7 grams protein, 165 milligrams sodium, 4 grams dietary fiber.

Eggs Head Back Up The Charts

Photo by David Eulitt • THE KANSAS CITY STAR

Like Humpty Dumpty, the egg's popularity has had a great fall.

Once upon a time, the egg was considered a smart, economical way to provide protein in the diet, along with essential vitamins and minerals. But then it fell from grace, a dastardly source of cholesterol and salmonella, a food-borne illness caused by undercooked eggs.

More recently, the lowly egg — in moderation — is getting the thumb's up. Not surprisingly, food manufacturers have found ways to pasteurize eggs so that they are cholesterol-free and free from salmonella.

If you haven't cracked yet, try the cholesterol-free, pasteurized egg product in *The Star's* Spinach Frittata. Pronounced frih-TAH-tuh, the meatless Italian-style omelet is versatile enough to serve for breakfast, lunch or dinner. The only difference from the traditional French omelet is a slightly firmer texture and no fold.

By using an egg product, we've removed some of the cholesterol. We also reduced the fat content by choosing a reduced-fat mozzarella made with part-skim milk.

Deep, leafy green spinach to add phytonutrients and plenty of vitamin C.

Spinach Frittata

Makes 4 servings

2 tablespoons butter
1/2 cup chopped onion
1 cup sliced fresh mushrooms
3 cups coarsely chopped fresh spinach
1 1/2 cups cholesterol-free egg product
1/4 teaspoon seasoned salt
1/2 teaspoon hot pepper sauce
2 green onions, chopped
2 tablespoons reduced-fat shredded mozzarella cheese
Prepared salsa for serving

Melt butter in 9- to 10-inch nonstick skillet over medium heat. Add onion and mushrooms and sauté until tender. Add spinach and cook, stirring frequently, just until wilted.

Stir together egg product, salt and hot pepper sauce; pour over spinach. Cook, covered, over low heat, until egg product is set, about 5 to 7 minutes. (Watch carefully, and lift edges of set egg product gently as needed to allow uncooked egg product to flow under cooked portion.) Garnish top with green onions and shredded mozzarella cheese. Cut into wedges to serve; garnish with salsa.

Per serving: 118 calories (49 percent from fat), 7 grams total fat (4 grams saturated), 17 milligrams cholesterol, 5 grams carbohydrates, 10 grams protein, 313 milligrams sodium, 1 gram dietary fiber.

Equipment Tip: No need for an omelet pan, but housewares stores now sell silicone spatulas that are heat-resistant up to 500 degrees and won't knick the finish on a nonstick skillet.

Tastes Like The Real Thing

If you think ordering a take-out pizza is faster than cooking at home, it's time to set the timer for a game of beat the clock. *The Star's* Pizza Pasta Salad comes together in the time it takes to boil water. Even better, the results are a dead ringer for the real thing.

The recipe starts with the ever-popular pizza flavor profile as cover to sneak in some vegetables. Spinach is not a great source of iron, but it does have loads of disease-fighting carotenoids and phytonutrients that help protect against cancer, high cholesterol and vision loss.

Tomatoes are high in vitamin C, as well as antioxidants beta-carotene, lutein and lycopene.

The Mushroom Council (mushroominfo.com) touts "nature's hidden treasure" as having fewer calories than a rice cake. Mushrooms also have zero grams of fat and several important nutrients, including the antioxidants ergothioneine and selenium, B vitamins, copper, phosphorous, potassium and vitamin D.

Next trade high-fat pepperoni for a combination of leaner turkey pepperoni and Canadian bacon. Canadian bacon is taken from the lean eye of loin.

And many pizzas are simply swimming in cheese. For a cheesy flavor with less fat, combine low-fat mozzarella and Parmesan, a hard, aged cheese that automatically contains less fat than, say, a creamy brie.

Finally, olive oil adds a heart-healthy fat to the traditional vinaigrette.

FEEDING A CROWD? This recipe makes enough for a meal with leftovers. It's also a good potluck or entertaining option.

Photo by David Eulitt • THE KANSAS CITY STAR

Pizza Pasta Salad

Makes 8 hearty main-dish servings

1 (16-ounce) package wagon wheel
   or fiori pasta
3 tomatoes, seeded and chopped
3 green onions, chopped
6 mushrooms, sliced
1 to 2 cups thinly sliced fresh spinach
3 ounces turkey pepperoni, thinly sliced
3 slices (3 ounces) Canadian bacon,
   cut into bite-size pieces
1/2 cup shredded low-fat mozzarella cheese
1/4 cup shredded Parmesan cheese
1 teaspoon Italian seasoning
1 teaspoon garlic salt
3 tablespoons tomato paste
1/4 cup red wine vinegar
7 tablespoons extra-virgin olive oil

Pump It Up: Choose multigrain pasta for extra fiber, B vitamins and phytonutrients.

Cook pasta according to package directions. Rinse under cold water; drain and place in a large salad bowl. Add tomatoes, green onions, mushrooms, spinach, pepperoni, Canadian bacon and cheeses; toss to combine.

Whisk together remaining ingredients and pour over pasta.

Serve immediately.

Per serving: 403 calories (37 percent from fat), 16 grams total fat (3 grams saturated), 18 milligrams cholesterol, 48 grams carbohydrates, 16 grams protein, 677 milligrams sodium, 3 grams dietary fiber.

SHOPPING TIPS: Tomato paste typically is high in sodium. If you wish to further reduce your sodium intake, look for a no-salt added version.

Canadian bacon is actually closer to ham than bacon. It's more expensive than bacon but leaner and precooked so there is no shrinkage. Look for it in the deli or the refrigerator case where cold cuts are sold.

Macaroni And Cheese, Please!

In 1937 Kraft introduced an instant version and an all-American comfort food was born. Rationing of meat and milk during World War II made the idea of meatless meals a winner.

So what about homemade versions?

I once found an Italian recipe version so unctuous it called for cooking the noodles in a gallon of whole milk. The recipe also called for fine, high-quality cheeses and a homemade bread crumb topping. But when I tried it out on my kids they said: "It's good, but not as good as the stuff in the box."

The only problem is a 7.25-ounce package of Kraft Macaroni & Cheese packs a whopping 18 grams of fat per serving. Not to mention artificial colors, like yellow No. 5 and yellow No. 6.

The Star's Slimmer Macaroni And Cheese contains skim milk and reduced-fat cheeses. Our remake of the classic convenience food clocks in at close to half the fat of the original.

PUMP IT UP: Try a wholegrain pasta. Or try some of the buckwheat, spelt and quinoa pastas available at health-food supermarkets.

Photo by David Eulitt • THE KANSAS CITY STAR

Slimmer Macaroni And Cheese

Makes 6 to 8 servings

3 tablespoons butter
6 tablespoons all-purpose flour
1 teaspoon dry mustard
1/2 teaspoon salt
1/8 teaspoon white or black pepper
3 cups fat-free skim milk, divided
1 1/4 cups shredded reduced-fat
    sharp cheddar cheese, divided
1/4 cup shredded reduced-fat Swiss cheese
1/4 cup shredded Parmesan cheese
5 cups cooked cavatappi pasta
    or large elbow macaroni

Preheat oven to 350 degrees. Melt butter in a large saucepan over medium heat. Stir in flour, mustard, salt and pepper. Gradually add 1 cup milk and stir with a whisk until smooth. Cook 1 minute, stirring constantly. Gradually add remaining 2 cups milk and cook 5 to 10 minutes or until slightly thick and bubbly, stirring constantly. Remove from heat and add 3/4 cup cheddar cheese, Swiss cheese and Parmesan cheese, stirring until cheese melts. Fold in cooked pasta.

Coat a 2-quart casserole with nonstick vegetable cooking spray. Pour pasta mixture into casserole. Top with remaining cheddar cheese. Cover and bake 30 minutes.

Stove-top method: If desired, prepare recipe as directed, reducing milk to 2 1/2 cups. Fold in cooked macaroni, as directed. Return to low heat and cook, stirring frequently, 5 to 10 minutes.

Per serving, based on 6: 351 calories (25 percent from fat), 10 grams total fat (6 grams saturated), 27 milligrams cholesterol, 46 grams carbohydrates, 19 grams protein, 513 milligrams sodium, 2 grams dietary fiber.

Shopping Tip: If your family is not already used to the taste, choose reduced-fat cheeses rather than a fat-free version.

Fast-Food Fave Gets A Remake

If there's a ubiquitous kiddie food in America, it has to be chicken nuggets.

Introduced by McDonald's in 1983, the breaded tenders are available everywhere from fast-food restaurants to school cafeterias to the family dinner table. Although they were introduced to satisfy the consumer's taste for healthier options, Chicken McNuggets contain twice as much fat per ounce as a hamburger, according to Eric Schlosser, author of *Fast Food Nation* (Harper Perennial).

The Star's Healthy Chicken Strips are baked to reduce the excess saturated fat added by deep-fat frying. The white meat remains moist with the addition of plain, lowfat yogurt sealed with a tasty cornflake crumb crust.

The next hurdle is to get the kids to skip the fries. Luckily most kids enjoy the sweetness and crunch of raw carrots. Carrots, of course, are one of the best sources of beta carotene and vitamin A, but they also contain plenty of fiber. Add raisins, green grapes and mix together with a low-fat yogurt for the added benefit of calcium.

Photo by David Eulitt • THE KANSAS CITY STAR

Healthy Chicken Strips

Makes 4 to 6 servings

2/3 cup Italian bread crumbs
1 cup cornflake crumbs
1/2 cup grated Parmesan cheese
2 cloves garlic, minced
Dash of salt
1 (8-ounce) carton plain low-fat yogurt
1 egg
1 to 1 1/2 pounds boneless, skinless chicken breasts, cut into strips

Preheat oven to 450 degrees. Line a baking sheet with aluminum foil and spray with nonstick vegetable cooking spray to coat.

In a bowl, combine bread crumbs, cornflake crumbs, Parmesan, garlic and salt; set aside. In another bowl, combine yogurt and egg; whisk to combine.

Dip chicken in yogurt mixture, then in the crumb mixture, turning to coat evenly. Place in a single layer on baking sheet. Spray tops of coated chicken strips with nonstick vegetable cooking spray. Bake 10 minutes; turn chicken strips over and spray tops again. Bake 10 minutes or until chicken is fully cooked and no longer pink.

Per serving, based on 4: 247 calories (15 percent from fat), 4 grams total fat (2 grams saturated), 95 milligrams cholesterol, 19 grams carbohydrates, 32 grams protein, 637 milligrams sodium, 1 gram dietary fiber.

Carrot Raisin Slaw

Makes 10 to 12 servings

4 cups shredded carrots or 1 (10-ounce) package shredded carrots
1 cup halved, seedless green grapes
1 teaspoon grated orange zest
1 orange, peeled and chopped
1 (6-ounce) container low-fat orange-flavored yogurt
1/4 teaspoon salt
Raisins, optional

Combine all ingredients except raisins; toss to coat carrots evenly with yogurt. Cover and refrigerate. To serve, spoon onto plate. Garnish with raisins, if desired.

Per serving, based on 10: 50 calories (5 percent from fat), trace fat (no saturated fat), 1 milligram cholesterol, 11 grams carbohydrates, 1 gram protein, 80 milligrams sodium, 2 grams dietary fiber.

Bowling For Flavor

Photo by David Eulitt • THE KANSAS CITY STAR

Throughout the fast-food industry, "bowl-based meals" are all the rage.

When Taco Bell began their bowl blitz, the company's executives launched a $20 million ad campaign based on extensive consumer research, according to *Restaurant Business*. Consumer research showed 84 percent prefer to eat with utensils rather than their hands and 93 percent eat out of bowls at least once a week.

Playing on this trend, *The Star's* Taco Pasta Bowls combine two ethnic-inspired flavors: Italian and Mexican. But, of course, the end result is an All-American dish.

A playful variation of macaroni and cheese with a little extra fiber thanks to the chili beans, savvy marketers say the way to get teens to try new things is to combine a familiar flavor with a new, unexpected flavor. The potential for experimentation with such bowl-based meals is limitless. Change the choice of bean, meat or cheese and you've got a slightly different bowl.

So what makes this homemade version healthier than fast-food bowls?

Instead of using a commercial taco seasoning mix, chili powder, garlic powder and cumin work well as a seasoning base and the savings in sodium is significant when you consider a 2-teaspoon serving of filling made with Lawry's Taco Spices and Seasonings contains 340 milligrams of sodium. The addition of no-salt added tomatoes also keeps the sodium at a more moderate level.

Taco Pasta Bowl

Makes 6 servings

1/2 pound ground round
1 (15.5-ounce) can chili beans (do not drain)
1 (10-ounce) can no-salt added diced tomatoes
2 ounces chopped green chilies
1 (10-ounce) can enchilada sauce
2 teaspoons chili powder
3/4 teaspoon cumin
1/2 teaspoon garlic powder
3 cups cooked pasta shells, such as cavatappi
   or large elbow
1 cup shredded Colby-Jack cheese
1/2 cup reduced-fat shredded sharp cheddar cheese

Cook ground round in a large skillet over medium-high heat, stirring to crumble; drain. Stir in chili beans, tomatoes, green chilies, enchilada sauce, chili powder, cumin and garlic powder. Simmer 3 to 5 minutes. Add pasta to mixture and heat 3 minutes. Stir in cheese until melted and well blended. Serve in bowls.

Per serving, based on 6: 357 calories (35 percent from fat), 14 grams total fat (6 grams saturated), 44 milligrams cholesterol, 38 grams carbohydrates, 18 grams protein, 480 milligrams sodium, 6 grams dietary fiber.

PUMP IT UP: Instead of regular pasta, upgrade to a wholegrain version for more fiber and health-promoting phytonutrients.

Instead of ground round, try leaner ground turkey or chicken.

Top bowl with lettuce or other leafy green and a fresh salsa. Add fruit and milk for a full meal deal.

Shopping Tips: Ground round is around 11 percent lean.

Be sure to read the nutrition label on enchilada sauce as sodium contents vary from brand to brand.

Lentils Full Of Fiber And Iron

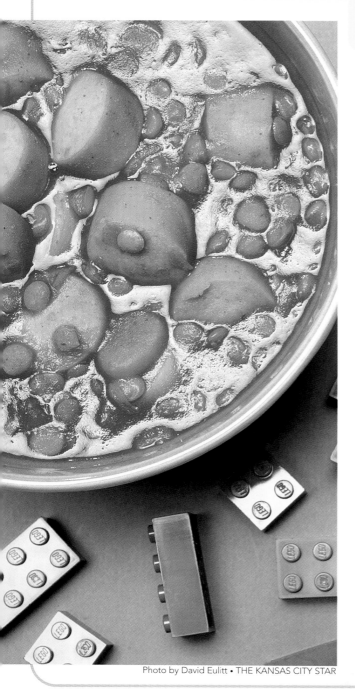

Think of lentils as the tiny, but mighty superheroes of the bean world.

The Star's kid-friendly version of Beans And Franks substitutes lentils for the baked beans typically found in a canned version of this dish.

Lentils are low in fat and rich in protein. But that's just for starters. They're also high in iron and cholesterol-lowering soluble fiber, and they're a good source of iron, phosphorous, potassium and calcium.

An average can of beans and franks have 17 grams of total fat (6 grams saturated) and over 1,000 milligrams of sodium, according to CalorieKing.com. Using low-fat beef franks and no-salt added tomato sauce helps lower those numbers.

But what really makes lentils an ideal kid food is they're also loaded with fiber. Since the American diet typically revolves around meat, eggs and dairy, only 39 percent of children ages 2 to 17 meet the USDA's dietary recommendation for fiber.

Fiber slows fat absorption, reduces cholesterol, promotes regularity and reduces the risk of some cancers. Fiber also makes us feel full which discourages overeating.

How much is enough?

For children over 2, try the "age plus 5 rule," according to kidshealth.org. Figure a 14-year-old would need $14 + 5 = 19$ grams of fiber per day. With this dish, you've already eaten nearly half your daily intake.

SHOPPING TIPS: Lentils are available in bags and in bulk bins. Although lentils can be stored in a cool, dry place for up to a year, it's best to shop at a store that you know has good turnover so they are fresh.

Heinz is the only brand of spicy ketchup we found on the market. Feel free to use another ketchup brand, although the taste as well as the nutritional analysis may be slightly altered.

Beans And Franks

Makes 8 (1-cup) servings

1 tablespoon vegetable oil
1/2 cup chopped onion
1/2 cup chopped celery
1/2 cup finely chopped carrots
2 cloves garlic, minced
4 1/2 cups water
1 1/4 cups dry lentils
1 (8-ounce) can no-salt added tomato sauce
1/3 cup Heinz spicy ketchup
2 tablespoons brown sugar
1 1/2 teaspoons chili powder
1/2 teaspoon salt
1 (14-ounce) package low-fat beef franks,
    cut into 1-inch pieces

Heat oil in Dutch oven over medium-high heat. Add onion, celery, carrots and garlic and cook, stirring frequently, until vegetables are tender. Stir in water and lentils. Cover, heat to boiling, reduce heat and simmer 1 hour or until lentils are tender.

Stir in tomato sauce, ketchup, brown sugar, chili powder, salt and franks. Cover and simmer 10 to 15 minutes, stirring occasionally.

Per serving: 264 calories (37 percent from fat), 11 grams total fat (3 grams saturated), 53 milligrams cholesterol, 26 grams carbohydrates, 16 grams protein, 681 milligrams sodium, 10 grams dietary fiber.

COOKING TIP: If you steer clear of dry beans because you have to soak them the night before, you're in luck: Lentils do not need lengthy soaking before cooking.

Pump It Up: Lentils are high in iron which makes them a good replacement for red meat. Substitute tofu dogs for low-fat beef franks and you've created a vegetarian meal with the benefits of healthful soy protein.

No Crying Over These Onions

Still resolved to strip your diet of excess? There's no need to cry just at the thought of indulging in a batch of *The Star's* Guilt-Free Onion Rings: Just swap the egg yolk and a seasoned flour mixture for a lighter breading of egg whites and crushed cornflakes, then bake instead of deep-fat frying.

But wait! The good-for-you health news doesn't end there.

A workhorse of the kitchen, onions are often overlooked as a source of phytonutrients—including flavonoids and more than 50 sulfur-containing chemical compounds—which may help protect against a host of medical conditions, including cardiovascular disease, inflammation and a variety of cancers.

As in most fruits and vegetables, the phytonutrients are concentrated in the skin and outer layers. Cut an onion and the cell walls will rupture, producing thiopropanal sulfoxide, a substance that gives them their pungent smell and the ability to irritate the eyes and make you blubber at the sink.

To get the maximum health benefits from onions let them sit for 5 to 10 minutes on the cutting board before cooking, according to *SuperFoods Healthstyle: Proven Strategies for Lifelong Health* by Steven Pratt (William Morrow). Heat breaks down the thiopropanal sulfoxide so you want it to become as concentrated as possible before cooking.

SHOPPING TIP: Although delicious, fresh sweet onions such as Vidalia, OSO and Walla Walla contain fewer flavonoids than yellow storage onions. Look for onions that have a tight neck and a crackly, shiny covering free of soft spots or blemishes.

Photo by Jim Barcus • THE KANSAS CITY STAR

Guilt-Free Onion Rings

Makes 4 servings

1/4 cup fine dry bread crumbs
1/4 cup finely crushed cornflakes
1/8 teaspoon salt
1/8 teaspoon cayenne pepper, optional
1 to 2 medium yellow onions,
    sliced 1/4-inch thick
    and separated into rings
2 slightly beaten egg whites

Preheat oven to 450 degrees. Spray a large baking sheet with nonstick vegetable cooking spray. In a shallow pie plate combine bread crumbs, cornflakes, salt and pepper. Dip onions into egg whites, then in crumb mixture. Arrange onion rings in a single layer on the prepared baking sheet. Spray onions with nonstick coating.

Bake 12 to 15 minutes or until the onions are tender and the coating is crisp and golden.

Per serving: 52 calories (7 percent from fat), trace total fat (no saturated fat), no cholesterol, 9 grams carbohydrates, 3 grams protein, 172 milligrams sodium, 1 gram dietary fiber.

COOKING TIPS: If onions make you tear up, try chilling them in the refrigerator for an hour before chopping. Allow the onions to come to room temperature and rest after cutting. (For rings, cut through the midsection instead of from root end to end.)

Use a food processor to crumb cornflakes to a fine coating.

You may need to prepare two baking sheets to hold all the onion rings.

Storage Tip: Do not store onions with potatoes; the spuds give off moisture, which spoils the onions.

Photo by Jill Toyoshiba • THE KANSAS CITY STAR

Onions Get A Thumbs Up

It's time for those golden globes.

OK, not those Golden Globes. This time the award goes to...the common onion.

With their yellow, red and white skins, globe onions may be ubiquitous, but they're certainly not past their prime. In fact, when it comes to nutrition, the onion triumvirate is truly cutting edge.

That's because onions contain quercetin, a flavonoid (one of a category of antioxidants) that may help prevent a host of common ailments ranging from cataracts to osteoporosis to cancer.

A study conducted at Wageningen Agricultural University in the Netherlands found the top dietary sources for quercetin are tea, onions and apples. But onions have twice the quercetin of tea and three times that of apples.

Coincidentally, onion consumption in the United States has risen 70 percent in the last two decades, from 12.2 pounds per person in 1983 to 21 pounds per person last year, the National Onion Association reports.

Onions were revered by ancient cultures for their healing powers, and Alexander the Great is reported to have fed his troops copious quantities to steel them for battle.

The onion's flavor, versatility and year-round availability have made it a culinary mainstay in nearly every major world cuisine. The Star's Grilled Steak Sandwich With Tri-Colored Onion Marmalade is a mouthwatering example of how a humble culinary staple can be transformed into something rich and memorable.

Granted, raw onions contain the most antioxidants, but the smooth, richness of caramelized onions reduced by slow cooking to a "marmalade" texture makes for a terrific condiment, as well as a natural complement to beef.

Once an overlooked cut, flank steak is high in zinc, iron and niacin. Just remember moderation; it gets nearly half its calories from fat.

Grilled Steak Sandwiches With Tri-Color Onion Marmalade

Makes 4 servings

1 pound beef flank steak
5 tablespoons orange juice, divided
2 tablespoons ketchup
2 tablespoon red wine vinegar
2 teaspoons Worcestershire sauce
3 cloves garlic, minced, divided
1/2 teaspoon pepper
1 1/2 cup chopped yellow sweet onion
1/4 cup chopped white onion
1/2 cup chopped red onion
1 teaspoon vegetable oil
1 tablespoon sugar
Salt and pepper to taste
4 whole-wheat hamburger buns, split and toasted

Pump It Up:

Here's an interesting fact for dinner conversation: Libya's average per capita consumption of onions is 66.8 pounds a year, the world's highest.

Place steak in zip-top plastic food bag. Combine 2 tablespoons orange juice, ketchup, red wine vinegar, Worcestershire sauce, 1 clove garlic and 1/2 teaspoon pepper. Pour over steak, seal bag and refrigerate several hours or overnight.

Preheat grill or allow coals to burn down to white ash. Drain steak and discard marinade. Grill steak 14 to 16 minutes or until meat thermometer registered 160 degrees for medium doneness, turning midway through cooking. Remove steak from grill, cover and allow to stand 5 minutes.

Place chopped onions and remaining garlic in small, heavy saucepan. Drizzle with oil and toss to coat evenly. Cook, stirring frequently, 5 minutes. Sprinkle with sugar, then add remaining 3 tablespoons orange juice.

Reduce heat to low and cook about 15 minutes or until golden brown and most of liquid has evaporated. Season lightly with salt and pepper. Remove form heat and allow to cool slightly.

Thinly slice steak, cutting across the grain. Cut steak strips into 1-inch pieces. Place steak strips on toasted buns and top each with onion marmalade.

Per serving: 433 calories (31 percent from fat), 15 grams total fat (8 grams saturated), 57 milligrams cholesterol, 45 grams carbohydrates, 30 grams protein, 424 milligrams sodium, 5 grams dietary fiber.

A Sweet (Potato) Solution

Photo by David Eulitt • THE KANSAS CITY STAR

Burgers and fries are a way of life with American teens, and it is taking its toll. Less than 40 percent teenagers meet the 2005 USDA's Dietary Guidelines fruit and vegetable intake.

And, no, ketchup is not considered a vegetable!

The Star's Baked Sweet Potato Fries offer at least two advantages over fast-food French fries. First, these sweet potato fries are baked in a small amount of olive oil, a monounsaturated or "good fat." Second, replacing white potatoes with sweet potatoes—one of the most nutrient-dense vegetables in the produce section—is a smart choice.

Sweet potatoes may help prevent cancer, degenerative eye disease, depression and heart disease. They are high in vitamins A and C, have a good amount of vitamin B and are rich in fiber.

Sweet potatoes are also loaded with beta-carotene, an antioxidant that is converted by the body into vitamin A. A "good" carb, sweet potatoes digest slowly, causing a gradual rise in blood sugar.

No wonder the Center for Science in the Public Interest rated the sweet potato as its number one vegetable. Naturally sweet as their name implies, sweet potatoes are relatively low in calories.

"I would definitely make these fries again because they were easy and something different," says Olivia Pusinelli, a 17-year-old student at Brookfield R-3 High School in Brookfield, Mo., who volunteered to test this recipe.

STORAGE TIP: Never refrigerate uncooked sweet potatoes; they lose their taste. Remove from plastic bag and store in a cool, dry place. Exposure to sunlight will make them sprout.

Baked Sweet Potato Fries

Makes 4 servings

2 large sweet potatoes
2 tablespoons olive oil
1/2 teaspoon salt
1/4 teaspoon pepper
1/4 teaspoon cayenne pepper, optional

Preheat oven to 400 degrees. Spray a baking sheet with nonstick vegetable cooking spray.

Peel potatoes, then cut into 1/4-by-2-inch strips. Place potato strips in a zip-top plastic food bag and drizzle with olive oil. Seal bag and shake to coat potatoes evenly. Spread in single layer on prepared baking sheet. Bake 15 minutes; stir gently, turning strips over. Bake 15 minutes; stir gently. Bake 5 to 10 minutes or until lightly brown. Season hot potatoes with salt, pepper and cayenne.

Per serving: 129 calories (48 percent from fat), 7 grams total fat (1 gram saturated), no cholesterol, 16 grams carbohydrates, 1 gram protein, 275 milligrams sodium, 2 grams dietary fiber.

COOKING TIP: You may use a vegetable peeler to remove the skin of sweet potatoes. Or eat them with their skins on for a dose of fiber that rivals oatmeal. But some sources recommend eating the skin only if the sweet potato has been organically grown.

Shopping Tip: The more orange the flesh, the more beta-carotene a sweet potato contains.

Classic Gets Healthful Tweaking

Baked beans are an all-American summer standby. Although a recipe for classic baked beans is simple —dried beans, water, salt, dry mustard, molasses, brown sugar and salt pork—that last ingredient typically sends the fat and sodium levels through the roof.

Jean Anderson, author of *The Nutrition Bible* (Morrow), estimates a serving of baked beans has nearly 400 calories, 13 grams of fat and more than 1,000 milligrams of sodium.

The Star's Picnic Beans makes several substitutions for the sake of nutrition and convenience in prepara-tion. For starters, use canned beans to eliminate the need for an overnight soaking. Then when it comes to flavoring the beans, skip the traditional salt pork in favor of leaner and less salty Canadian bacon and no-salt-added tomato sauce.

Beans are not only economical for large gatherings such as potlucks and picnics, they're also loaded with soluble fiber, an important factor in lowering LDL cholesterol. A complex carbohydrate, beans satisfy the appetite longer by allowing a slow, steady rise in blood-glucose levels.

Picnic Beans

Makes 12 servings

2 slices (1 ounce each) Canadian bacon,
  chopped
2/3 cup chopped onion
1 (16-ounce) can black beans,
  rinsed and drained
1 (16-ounce) can light red beans,
  rinsed and drained
1 (16-ounce) can pinto beans,
  rinsed and drained
1 (16-ounce) can Great Northern beans,
  rinsed and drained
2 (8-ounce) cans no-salt-added tomato sauce
1/4 cup cider vinegar
3 tablespoons molasses
1/4 cup brown sugar
1 teaspoon chili powder

Preparation Tip: Rinsing canned beans washes away 23 percent to 45 percent of the sodium added during processing.

Place Canadian bacon and onion in a nonstick skillet. Cook over medium-low heat, stirring frequently, until onions are tender and edges of bacon are lightly browned.

Place beans in mixing bowl. Add Canadian bacon-onion mixture. Combine remaining ingredients and pour over beans; stir to blend. Spoon into 2-quart baking dish.

Bake, uncovered, at 350 degrees, 45 to 60 minutes.

Per serving: 185 calories (5 percent from fat), 1 gram total fat (trace saturated fat), 2 milligrams cholesterol, 34 grams carbohydrates, 10 grams protein, 322 milligrams sodium, 8 grams dietary fiber.

SHOPPING TIPS: The combination of beans in this recipe is attractive, but you may choose all one type, or mix and match various types to suit your family's tastes.

When choosing molasses, the labels can be confusing: There are light (mild), dark and blackstrap versions. Blackstrap molasses usually includes nutrition labeling touting its superior health qualities. All molasses contains iron, calcium and phosphorus, although blackstrap generally has a more bitter aftertaste.

Broccoli Has Super Powers

Photo by David Eulitt • THE KANSAS CITY STAR

President Bush the Elder may not be a fan, but broccoli is a super power to be reckoned with.

High in phytonutrients such as beta-carotene, lutein, indoles and sulforaphane which may prevent various types of cancer, broccoli is also a good source of non-dairy source of calcium.

The Star's Broccoli Asian Noodle Slaw features a product called broccoli slaw. A relatively recent addition to the produce section, broccoli slaw is proof that not all convenience foods are bad for you. The shredded stalks are preshredded and tossed with flecks of purple cabbage and tiny threads of carrot.

Another convenience food that often takes a hit from nutritionists is ramen-style soups because the noodles are fried and the seasoning packets are high in sodium. Instead, look for chukka soba, an Asian curly noodle product that is baked. Skip the seasoning packet in favor of a light ginger-soy sauce and a few noodles.

The result is a lighter version of a popular potluck side. To further enhance the flavor profile and nutritional content, add a sprinkling of toasted walnuts. Nuts of all varieties have long received a bad rap with dieters. However, new research shows they are rich in phytonutrients and heart-healthy monounsaturated fat. Walnuts, in particular, have been found to contain more omega-3 fatty acids than fish. Omega-3 fatty acids may lower the risk of heart attack and stroke.

Even though the percentage of calories from fat is higher than the 30 percent or less recommended, it's important to note the types of fat—mono- and polyunsaturated—which are good for the heart and may also reduce the risk of certain types of cancer. The amount of total fat per serving is low.

Broccoli Asian Noodle Slaw

Makes 12 servings

1 (3-ounce) package Japanese curly noodles
  (chukka soba)
4 cups broccoli slaw
1 carrot, shredded
1 green pepper, chopped
2 tablespoons canola oil
3 tablespoons white wine vinegar
3 tablespoons sugar
3 tablespoons reduced-sodium soy sauce
1 teaspoon grated fresh ginger
2 cloves garlic
1/4 cup chopped walnuts, toasted

Crumble uncooked noodles into salad bowl. Add broccoli slaw, carrot and green pepper.

Whisk together oil, vinegar, sugar, soy sauce, ginger and garlic; pour over slaw and toss to coat well. Top with walnuts just before serving.

Per serving: 72 calories (50 percent from fat), 4 grams total fat (trace saturated fat), no cholesterol, 7 grams carbohydrates, 2 grams protein, 159 milligrams sodium, 1 gram dietary fiber.

PUMP IT UP: For a heartier main dish salad, added cooked, diced chicken breast or leftover shrimp.

TO TOAST NUTS: Place chopped walnuts on baking tray. Bake at 350 degrees about 7 minutes or until lightly toasted.

Shopping Tip: Look for chukka soba in the same aisle as the ramen at well-stocked supermarkets. You can also find them at ethnic groceries.

Some Assembly Required

My editor doesn't cook. Her oven serves as a makeshift pantry to stash the dog's food.

Sound extreme? Not so much. Her "I-am-no-domestic-goddess" attitude has become not only feasible but downright fashionable.

From rotisserie chicken to sushi, frozen pizza to microwave burritos, there's no denying Americans are cooking less and assembling more.

These prepared foods seem the perfect shortcut when you need dinner on the table in a hurry.

Often the trade-off for convenience is a diet that is high in sodium.

Consider the wrap sandwich, a fast-food favorite that has the aura of health—until you consider a grilled chicken wrap from Sonic (sonicdrivein.com/pdfs/menu/SonicNutritionGuide) has 539 calories, 27 grams of fat and a whopping 1,035 milligrams of sodium. Skip the ranch dressing to get it down to 393 calories, 12 grams of fat and 820 milligrams of sodium.

A Google search turns up a host of chicken wraps with similar sodium stats. For instance, at calorie-count.com, the Arby's Low Carbys Chicken Caesar Wrap receives a nutrition grade of C+. Not all bad. It's low in sugar, very high in dietary fiber, high in protein. Ah, but it also has—ouch!—1,530 milligrams of sodium, more than half your daily allotment.

Most American diets are out of whack when it comes to sodium. The recommended daily intake for salt is no more than 2,400 milligrams, or about a teaspoon of salt.

By assembling The Star's Asian Chicken Salad Wraps at home, you can replace the popular Caesar dressing with a vinaigrette to cut the sodium as well as additional fat and calories.

To pump up the nutrition, add more variety to your salad by including darker greens such as spinach and more color with carrots, tomatoes, red peppers and onions.

Asian Chicken Wraps

Makes 6 to 8 servings

3 tablespoons red wine vinegar
1 tablespoon honey
1 tablespoon reduced-sodium soy sauce
1 teaspoon grated fresh ginger
1/2 teaspoon sesame oil
1/4 teaspoon crushed red pepper flakes
1 clove garlic, minced
Salt and pepper to taste
1 1/2 cups chopped, cooked skinless
    rotisserie chicken
3 cups torn romaine
1 cup torn fresh spinach
1 large carrot, shredded (about 1 cup)
1 Roma tomato, seeded and chopped
1/2 cup chopped red pepper
2 green onions, chopped
2 tablespoons minced fresh cilantro
6 to 8 low-fat wheat tortillas

Shopping Tip: Feel free to substitute other flavors of low-fat tortillas, including honey wheat, spinach and vegetable or sun-dried tomato and basil.

Combine vinegar, honey, soy sauce, ginger, sesame oil, red pepper flakes and garlic. Season lightly with salt and pepper; set aside.

Toss together chicken, romaine, spinach, carrot, tomato, red pepper, green onion and cilantro. Drizzle with dressing mixture and toss to coat.

Wrap each tortilla in a damp paper power and microwave on high (100 percent) about 20 seconds or just until warm.

Spoon salad mixture into center of warm tortilla, then fold tortilla over filling.

Per serving, based on 6: 149 calories (12 percent from fat), 2 grams total fat (trace saturated), trace cholesterol, 32 grams carbohydrates, 5 grams protein, 253 milligrams sodium, 3 grams dietary fiber.

STORAGE TIP: For nights when you're tempted to resort to a frozen microwave entrée, keep tortillas at the ready in the freezer. To avoid ripping and tearing tortillas off the block, here's a tip from *The Best Kitchen Quick Tips by Cook's Illustrated*: Place each tortilla between sheets of wax or parchment paper. Place the stack in a freezer bag and freeze as usual.

Calzones Offer Portion Control

Photo by Tammy Ljungblad • THE KANSAS CITY STAR

On the face of it, a veggie pizza seems like a healthy choice.

That is until you've wolfed down an overly cheesy pie the size of the moon.

Enter the calzone—a good choice for health-minded pizza lovers who might be tempted to eat the whole thing. Originally from Naples, a calzone automatically limits you to an individual portion size and cuts down on the need for excess cheese.

A few years ago, the watchdog nutrition group Center for Science in the Public Interest measured the impact of the $30 billion pizza industry on America's bulging waistline and found it to be significant.

Just one slice of Pizza Hut's Stuffed-Crust Meat Lover's Pizza is equivalent to a McDonald's Quarter Pounder, and one slice of Pizza Hut's Big New Yorker Sausage pizza has more fat than a McDonald's Big Mac.

"While most people wouldn't unwrap and eat a second Quarter Pounder or Big Mac, many people reach for a second, third, or even a fourth slice of their favorite pizza," CSPI's report concludes.

In addition to promoting portion control, *The Star's* Vegetable Calzones offer a substantial helping of veggies.

Mushrooms are loaded with B vitamins and selenium, an antioxidant mineral that may protect against cancer and macular degeneration.

Spinach packs a wallop with disease-fighting carotenoids.

Canned tomatoes in the sauce are a great source of lycopene, an antioxidant that prevents cell damage.

Vegetable Calzones

Makes 4 servings

1 teaspoon olive oil
1/2 cup chopped onion
2 cloves garlic, minced
1/2 cup sliced mushrooms
3 Roma tomatoes, seeded and chopped
3/4 cup coarsely chopped fresh spinach leaves
2/3 cup pizza sauce
1/2 teaspoon dried oregano leaves
1 (13.8-ounce) tube refrigerated pizza crust
1/2 to 3/4 cup shredded part-skim mozzarella cheese
1/4 cup grated Parmesan cheese

Preheat oven to 400 degrees. Heat olive oil in medium-size skillet over medium-high heat. Add onion and garlic and cook, stirring frequently, until onion is tender. Add mushrooms and cook, stirring frequently, 2 to 3 minutes. Stir in Roma tomatoes and cook, stirring frequently, 1 minute. Stir in spinach and cook just until spinach wilts. Stir in pizza sauce.

Cut log of pizza dough into fourths. Using the heel of your hand, press each part into a circle about 7- to 7 1/2-inches in diameter on lightly floured board. (You may also use a lightly floured rolling pin.) Spray a large baking sheet with nonstick vegetable cooking spray. Place dough circles on prepared pan. Top each with 2 to 3 tablespoons mozzarella cheese and 1 tablespoon Parmesan. Spoon 1/4 of vegetable mixture into center of each. Gently fold half of dough over filling and press edges to seal. Bake 10 to 15 minutes or until golden brown.

Per serving: 391 calories (24 percent from fat), 10 grams total fat (3 grams saturated), 12 milligrams cholesterol, 58 grams carbohydrates, 17 grams protein, 896 milligrams sodium, 2 grams dietary fiber.

Shopping Tip: This recipe uses a tube of refrigerator pizza crust to turn out a quick, delicious crust. In addition to convenience, the ready-to-bake dough eliminates the need to deep fry or brush the crust with olive oil like some commercially made calzones. Look for tubes of it the refrigerated cases, usually near the cookies and biscuits.

Photo by Rich Sugg • THE KANSAS CITY STAR

Healthy Can Be Gourmet

Clever chefs know how to turn a traditional dish on its head.

In recent years, diners with a taste for the eclectic have winked right along as these culinary wizards have deconstructed campfire s'mores, gussied up plain-jane corn grits with goat cheese, turned grilled cheese into a gourmet delicacy on a platform of artisan bread and whipped up such unlikely odd couples as foie gras and cappuccino.

But home cooks can be every bit as clever when they put their minds to it.

The Star's Not-Your-Mother's Tuna Salad Sandwich has all the traditional components of tuna salad—tuna, mayonnaise, bread and lettuce—just in a different presentation.

The first step is to abandon the can and rely on the intense flavor of fresh tuna steaks. Once they're lightly seared on the grill, each steak is placed on a slice of whole-grain toast and smeared with a half-and-half spread made of fat-free mayo and plain low-fat yogurt.

To heighten the fresh flavor, the creamy spread is spiked with plenty of fresh basil and lime juice. The open-face sandwich is topped with a heap of deep green lettuces lightly dressed in a balsamic vinaigrette. It's a playful rendition of "tuna salad"—one sure to make even the most jaded mom smile.

Not-Your-Mother's Tuna Salad Sandwich

Makes 4 servings

4 tuna steaks, about 3 to 4 ounces each
Juice of 1 lime
2 tablespoons chopped fresh basil, divided
2 tablespoons fat-free mayonnaise
2 tablespoons low-fat plain yogurt
Grated zest of 1 lime
4 cups fresh torn salad greens or spinach
2 tablespoons balsamic vinegar
1 tablespoon olive oil
1 teaspoon honey
Salt and pepper to taste
4 slices whole-grain or whole-wheat bread, toasted

Cooking Tip: Serve tuna charred on the outside and rare in the center; it dries out when overcooked.

Place tuna in zip-top plastic food bag. Drizzle with lime juice and sprinkle with 1 tablespoon basil. Seal bag and allow to stand 10 to 15 minutes. Preheat grill or allow to burn down to white ash. Away from the flame, spray grill rack pan with nonstick vegetable cooking spray. Grill steaks about 4 to 5 minutes per side, preferably rare, or until done as desired and fish flakes easily with a fork; do not overcook or the fish will dry out.

Meanwhile, in a small bowl, combine mayonnaise, yogurt, zest of lime and remaining tablespoon basil; blend well.

Place salad greens in a mixing bowl. Combine balsamic vinegar, oil, honey, salt and pepper; drizzle over greens and toss to coat well.

To serve, spread one side of each slice of toast with about 1 tablespoon mayonnaise mixture and place, spread side up, on dinner plate. Top with tuna steak, then about 1/4 of salad mixture.

Per serving: 257 calories (31 percent from fat), 9 grams total fat (2 grams saturated), 33 milligrams cholesterol, 21 grams carbohydrates, 25 grams protein, 295 milligrams sodium, 4 grams dietary fiber.

SHOPPING TIP: Fresh and frozen tuna, like swordfish, is considered high in methylmercury. In general, smaller fish have less mercury (including canned tuna). For most people, the health benefits appear to outweigh the risks of methylmercury, if tuna is eaten no more than once a week.

Photo by Tammy Ljungblad • THE KANSAS CITY STAR

Good Nutrition On The Go

Sure, fried chicken, potato salad and coleslaw are considered your standard, all-American picnic fare. But the movable feast begs a few modern questions: Is it lean? Is it convenient to make? And, once you make it, is it easily portable to your rendezvous site?

Looks like it's time to take a cue from the French. When heading for a grassy knoll under a shady tree, they tote along tuna pan bagnat (pronounced "pan ban-YAH").

A sandwich is by definition easy to make and easily portable. The Star's version of Tuna Pan Bagnat is the perfect picnic sandwich because it must be made ahead of time.

The name means "soaked bread." In this case, a very crusty baguette is the perfect bread to use. The top and bottom slices are painted with olive oil, a heart-healthy monounsaturated fat that keeps water-packed tuna, which has the tendency to be mealy or dry, moist. The sandwich ingredients—lean protein paired with antioxidant-rich tomatoes, onions, spinach and peppers—are also bathed in a white wine vinaigrette.

The idea is the flavors seep into the bread as it is pressed. Luckily no fancy equipment is required. To press it, simply place a narrow tray, small skillet or a couple of small plates on top of the sandwich, and then weigh that down with a can from the pantry.

Tuna Pan Bagnat

Makes 6 servings

1 very crusty baguette
2 tablespoons white wine vinegar
2 teaspoons olive oil
2 cloves garlic, minced
Freshly ground pepper to taste
16 to 20 fresh small spinach or lettuce leaves, trimmed
1 (6-ounce) can chunk white tuna in water,
    drained and flaked
1/2 cup shredded mozzarella cheese
1/4 cup finely chopped red onion
3 Roma tomatoes, thinly sliced
1/2 small red pepper, very thinly sliced
3/4 to 1 cup very thin slices cucumber

Split baguette in half lengthwise. With fingertips, gently scoop out soft center of each bread half, leaving a shell. (Reserve soft bread for other use.) Place bread shells, cut side up, on large sheet of heavy-duty aluminum foil. Combine wine vinegar, olive oil, garlic and pepper. Brush cut surface of bread with vinegar mixture; reserve remaining vinegar mixture.

Arrange half of spinach leaves in a single layer in one bread shell. Spoon tuna evenly down center of bread shell on top of spinach leaves. Layer, in order, over tuna: shredded cheese, onion, tomatoes and red pepper. Slowly drizzle with remaining vinegar mixture, pouring so that it soaks down over vegetables in sandwich. Arrange cucumbers (overlapping as necessary) over sandwich, then place remaining spinach leaves on top of cucumber. Top sandwich with second bread shell.

Wrap sandwich very tightly in aluminum foil. Place on tray. Weigh down top of sandwich. Refrigerate 2 to 24 hours.

Per serving: 307 calories (19 percent from fat), 7 grams total fat (2 grams saturated), 17 milligrams cholesterol, 45 grams carbohydrates, 17 grams protein, 604 milligrams sodium, 4 grams dietary fiber.

Shopping Tip: Be sure to use very crusty bread, such as a day-old baguette.

Lean And Mean Taco Salad

Who invented the taco salad?

Credit appears to go to Mr. Giant Salad Inventor. He's the hapless dude on the Anheuser-Busch "Real Men" commercials who parodies the now-ubiquitous Tex-Mex innovation—essentially the high-calorie contents of a taco spilled onto a bed of lettuce.

Cute, but everybody knows adding a few shreds of iceberg lettuce doesn't take it out of the category of dubious diet fare.

But with a few simple tweaks, *The Star's* Fiesta Salad turns the fast-food staple into something slimmer and trimmer:

• Go beyond iceberg: As a rule, the richer the color, the more vitamins and minerals lettuce contains. Skip the iceberg and go for romaine, Boston, bibb and Oak Leaf. The addition of dark green spinach, a rich source of iron and vitamins A and C, also significantly ups the nutrient content.

• Keep the crunch: As the taco shell moved north of the border, the soft corn tortilla got deep-fried, a cooking method that adds saturated fat and calories. For the same crunch, grab a bag of baked tortilla chips.

• Choose lean protein: Instead of ground beef, use baked chicken strips.

• Boost fiber and flavor: There's nothing wrong with adding high-quality convenience foods to your repertoire. We like the mixture of black beans, corn, roasted red peppers, onions and chilies in our frozen food section. For testing purposes we used C&W brand, but any similar Southwestern-style mixture will do.

Photo by David Eulitt • THE KANSAS CITY STAR

Fiesta Taco Salad

Makes 6 servings

1 pound boneless, skinless
    chicken breast halves
1/2 teaspoon salt
1/2 teaspoon pepper
1 teaspoon chili powder
8 cups torn lettuce leaves
    (or one 11-ounce package
    prepared salad greens)
2 cups torn spinach leaves
1 large carrot, shredded
2 Roma tomatoes, seeded and chopped
1 (14-ounce) package frozen
    Southwest blend of corn, black beans,
    poblano chilies, roasted red pepper
    and onion, thawed and drained
1/2 cup reduced-fat shredded cheddar cheese
1/2 cup baked tortilla chips or corn chips,
    coarsely crushed
1/2 cup fat-free ranch dressing
1/4 cup salsa

Shopping Tip: Consider using a reduced-fat cheese. If you thought they tasted rubbery and bland, it might be time to try again; reduced-fat cheeses have improved in recent years.

Place chicken breasts in 9-by-13-inch baking dish and spray each side with nonstick vegetable cooking spray. Combine salt, pepper and chili powder, and sprinkle over both sides of chicken. Bake at 425 degrees 25 to 30 minutes or until chicken is fully cooked and the internal temperature reaches 170 degrees. Set aside to cool slightly. Toss together lettuce, spinach, carrot, tomatoes and Southwest blend in large salad bowl. Cut chicken into thin strips and arrange over salad. Top with cheese and tortilla chips. Blend ranch dressing and salsa and serve with salad.

Per serving: 286 calories (10 percent from fat), 3 grams total fat (1 gram saturated), 46 milligrams cholesterol, 39 grams carbohydrates, 26 grams protein, 672 milligrams sodium, 5 grams dietary fiber.

LEARN TO SALSA: Skip the guacamole, sour cream and salad dressings that can add a lot of fat and empty calories to a salad. Instead try fat-free ranch salad dressing mixed with a sassy salsa to provide a flavorful flourish that's easier on your waistline.

A Mediterranean Spin On Tacos

Photo by Tammy Ljungblad • THE KANSAS CITY STAR

Thai chicken pizza, tandoori burritos and Cajun pasta are part of the American melting pot.

When two distinct ethnic food influences collide to create a hybrid dish, chefs call it fusion cuisine. The fusion doesn't necessarily mean it's lean, but it does provide a nice jumping-off point for creative cooks to take something familiar and turn it into something new by making a few healthy substitutions.

The Star's Greek Tacos take the standard Mexican-style taco—a hard or soft shell stuffed with ground meat and layered with lettuce, tomato and cheese—and gives it a spin using a whole-wheat pita. Puffy mini pitas are a great way to exercise portion control, but if you can't find these small flatbreads, a regular flat whole-wheat pita will work.

At the meat counter, choose lean ground round. Hamburger can contain up to 30 percent fat, but ground round contains no more than 15 percent fat, and in some cases as little as 5 percent fat.

Less fat can mean less flavor, but choosing assertive condiments will trick your taste buds. Choose a sprinkling of Greek feta instead of a mound of cheddar and a dollop of low-fat yogurt dill sauce instead of sour cream.

Finally, instead of iceberg lettuce, opt for spinach, a darker green with far more nutritional punch. Add grape tomatoes and a dose of beta-carotene, lutein, zeaxanthin and lycopene, antioxidants that may protect against cancer, heart disease and vision loss.

Greek Tacos

Makes 6 servings

1 pound ground round
1/2 cup chopped onion
2 garlic cloves, minced
2 teaspoons all-purpose Greek seasoning
1 1/2 teaspoons ground cumin
Salt and pepper to taste
1/2 cup grape or cherry tomatoes, cut into
    halves or fourths
1 cup fresh spinach, stems removed and discarded
6 mini whole-wheat pocket breads
Yogurt Dill Sauce (See recipe below)
3 tablespoons feta cheese

Cook ground round, onions and garlic in skillet over medium-high heat, stirring frequently, until beef is browned; drain well. Add Greek seasoning, cumin, salt and pepper and blend well.

Stir in tomatoes and spinach and cook over medium heat 3 to 5 minutes to allow tomatoes to become juicy and spinach to soften.

Cut pocket breads in half, then spoon mixture into each bread pocket and top with Yogurt Dill Sauce. Sprinkle sparingly with feta cheese.

Yogurt Dill Sauce: Blend together 1/2 cup nonfat plain yogurt, 1 teaspoon lemon juice and 1 teaspoon dried dillweed.

Per serving: 207 calories (23 percent from fat), 5 grams total fat (2 grams saturated), 45 milligrams cholesterol, 19 grams carbohydrates, 21 grams protein, 231 milligrams sodium, 2 grams dietary fiber.

SHOPPING TIPS: For testing Father Sam's brand mini wheat pita pockets were used. You can also use regular-size pitas (4 for 4 servings) or serve in taco shells (8 for 4 servings).

Shopping Tips: This recipe was tested with Cavender's Greek Seasoning, a blend of 13 ingredients. You can buy the seasoning blend online at Jane's Kitchen, cavendersseasoning.com.

A Kernel Of Truth

POPCORN IS A WHOLE GRAIN!

Stop the presses.

Is it true I can figure a 3-cup serving counts as one of three daily servings of whole grains?

Yep, says the USDA.

But, says Dan O'Connor, director of marketing for Orville Redenbacher: "Over 90 percent of people didn't realize popcorn is a whole grain. That really kind of told us we should get an education program out there."

An all-American snack food, plain popcorn has long been a diet strategy because the grain's dietary fiber is filling and helps keep blood sugar levels stable. But for me it's always been the equivalent of rice cakes. Filling, yes, but sadly no more satisfying than chewing on air.

I know. You can't lose weight if you sit in front of the TV munching popcorn loaded up with copious amounts of butter and more than a shake of salt. Likewise, jawing on caramel-coated popcorn can set you back as much as 400 calories per serving.

The good news?

Popcorn doesn't have to be bland to retain its nutritional value. *The Star's* Rosemary Cheese Popcorn adds enough flavor to pump up plain popcorn. In this case, the Parmesan cheese offers enough flavor to keep you from grabbing for the salt shaker while the rosemary gives off a terrific aroma and provides a wonderful, fresh flavor.

Popcorn adds phytonutrients, B vitamins and a healthy dose of fiber to the diet. Figure about 4 grams per serving. The average American eats about 10 grams of fiber but should be getting closer to 20 to 30 grams a day.

Rosemary Cheese Popcorn

Makes 8 to 10 cups

8 to 10 cups popped 94 percent fat-free
  microwave popcorn
1 tablespoon butter
1 tablespoon chopped fresh rosemary
  or 1 1/2 teaspoons crushed
  dried rosemary
3 tablespoons shredded Parmesan cheese

Storage Tip: Fresh rosemary lasts two to three weeks in the produce bin of the refrigerator.

Combine all ingredients in a plastic 2 1/2 gallon zip-top plastic food bag; shake vigorously to coat well.

Per (1-cup) cup, based on 8: 38 calories (49 percent from fat), 2 grams total fat (1 gram saturated), 5 milligrams cholesterol, 4 grams carbohydrates, 1 gram protein, 85 milligrams sodium, 1 gram dietary fiber.

SHOPPING TIP: Not all microwave popcorn is created equal so be sure to read the labels. To keep the fat content down, the American Institute of Cancer Research recommends buying "light" and "smart" styles which may have 40 to 60 calories and just 2 grams of fat as opposed to "theater-style" which is often drenched in butter and may contain 120 to 140 calories and 8 to 10 grams of fat. Also, be sure to avoid brands that contain hydrogenated vegetable oils, which add trans fats to the diet.

PREPARATION TIP: To pluck fresh rosemary, run your thumb and fore-finger from tip to stem. Spray knife with vegetables cooking spray to prevent the needles from sticking to the blade as you chop.

Thumbs Up For Green Tea

Photo by Rich Sugg • THE KANSAS CITY STAR

Throughout the day, beverages can add a substantial chunk of calories to the American diet.

Drinks high in calories, fat or sugar can contribute to obesity, tooth decay and a variety of other health problems.

The USDA's MyPyramid encourages consumers to choose beverages and foods to moderate their intake of sugar.

The Star's Raspberry Green Tea Cooler is a tasty blend that combines the tart taste of cranberries with cool green tea for a low-calorie, antioxidant-packed end-of-summer cooler.

Choosing beverages wisely can make the difference between a balanced diet and one that is out of whack. A 12-ounce can of regular soda adds 120 to 140 calories and zero nutrients to the diet. Although 100-percent fruit juices are a more healthful choice, they can also tally up calories quickly. For instance, 1 cup of cranberry juice cocktail with sugar contains 147 calories, although lighter juice versions with artificial sweeteners are available.

In search of a zero-calorie refresher, many Americans have learned to guzzle unsweetened iced tea on a regular basis. In fact, 40 billion of the 50 billion cups of tea consumed each year in this country are served over ice, according to the Tea Council.

If you're looking for zero calories and possible health benefits, green tea trumps iced tea. Not only is it rarely served with milk or sugar, it contains powerful antioxidants known as polyphenols, which may help prevent some types of cancer.

Green tea has roughly 30 percent to 40 percent polyphenols, while black tea contains just 3 percent to 10 percent polyphenols. The average cup of green tea contains 50 to 150 milligrams of polyphenols, according to the University of Maryland Medical Center.

Raspberry
Green Tea Cooler

Makes 4 servings (1 1/4 cups each)

2 raspberry green tea bags
1 cup light cranberry juice cocktail
2 cups 0-calorie raspberry sparkling water
Fresh raspberries for garnish
Slice of lime for garnish

Heat 1 cup water to a boil. Add tea bags and allow to steep 3 to 5 minutes. Pour into a pitcher and add 1 additional cup of water. Add cranberry juice cocktail and raspberry sparkling water. Serve with ice and if desired, float a few fresh raspberries in glass with a wedge of lime.

Per serving: 18 calories (none from fat), no fat, no cholesterol, 4 grams carbohydrates, trace protein, 5 milligrams sodium, no dietary fiber.

COOKING TIP: This recipe was tested using Celestial Seasonings raspberry-flavored green tea and Ocean Spray light cranberry juice cocktail, which has 40 calories per 1 cup serving.

Pump It Up: Cranberries have been shown to protect against urinary tract infections.

Healthy
Desserts

5

Satisfy Your Urge To Splurge

Are you cuckoo for cream puffs?
With some savvy ingredient substitutions, the miniature pastries are the perfect splurge for Easter brunch.

Cream puffs are made from pâte à choux (pronounced "shoo"). That's French for a simple mixture of boiling water, flour and butter.

Unlike other pastry doughs, choux is cooked on the stovetop to create a sticky mixture that is enriched with eggs. When baked, the eggs make the dough puff, creating a hollow middle.

Now before you go telling your guests that cream puffs have been declared a health food, consider the source. A basic recipe in *The Joy of Cooking* includes a stick of butter, 1/2 cup of whole milk and 4 whole eggs.

But *The Star's* recipe for Cream Puffs reduces the butter to just 3 tablespoons, skips the milk altogether and uses a mixture of whole eggs and egg whites.

In contrast, *Joy's* cream filling includes four egg yolks and milk.

Using an egg substitute and skim milk instead substantially reduces total calories, fat and cholesterol.

SERVING TIPS: You may prefer making the cavity of the cream puff slightly larger by gently pulling out some of the inner, softer dough, then filling as directed.

For a unique presentation, layer filling and puffs in a parfait glass.

Garnish top of parfait with chocolate and, if desired, add fresh berries and a mint leaf.

Cream Puffs

Makes 12 servings

Cooking Tip: Use the microwave to prepare the filling and spend less time stirring.

Cream filling:
1/3 cup all-purpose flour
1/2 cup sugar
1/8 teaspoon salt
2 cups fat-free skim milk, divided
1/4 cup egg substitute
1 1/2 teaspoons vanilla

Pastry shells:
1 cup water
3 tablespoons butter
2 teaspoons sugar
1/4 teaspoon salt
1 cup all-purpose flour
2 large eggs
2 large egg whites

Glaze:
2 tablespoons cocoa
1/4 teaspoon vanilla extracts
2/3 cup confectioners' sugar
2 tablespoons hot water
Optional garnish:
    Fresh berries and mint leaves

For cream filling: Place flour, sugar, salt and 1 3/4 cups milk in a medium microwavable bowl. Whisk well. Microwave on high 4 to 5 minutes or until thick, stirring every minute. Combine remaining 1/4 cup milk and egg substitute in a large bowl. Stir 1/4 of hot mixture into egg mixture and then blend all of egg mixture into remaining hot mixture. Microwave on high 1 minute; stir well. Stir in vanilla. Cover with plastic wrap, gently pressing plastic wrap down directly onto surface of pudding. Refrigerate at least 1 hour or until chilled. (Makes 2 1/2 cups.)

For pastry shells: Preheat oven to 425 degrees. Cover baking sheet with parchment paper or a silicone baking mat. Combine water, butter, sugar and salt in heavy saucepan. Heat over medium-high heat, stirring frequently with a wooden spoon, until mixture comes to a boil; remove from heat. Add flour, stirring well until mixture is smooth and pulls away from sides of pan. Return pan to heat and cook 30 seconds. Remove from heat and add eggs and egg whites, one at a time, beating with a mixer at medium speed until just combined. Continue beating 1 minute. Drop the dough into 12 mounds (scant 1/4 cup) about 2 inches apart on baking sheet. Bake 20 minutes. Cool completely on a rack.

For glaze: In a small bowl mix together cocoa, vanilla and confectioners' sugar. Stir in hot water to make thin glaze. Set aside.

To assemble: Cut top third from each shell. Divide filling among shells; replace top. Drizzle with glaze. Garnish with fresh berries and mint, if desired.

Per serving, based on 12: 178 calories (23 percent from fat), 5 grams total fat (2 grams saturated), 45 milligrams cholesterol, 29 grams carbohydrates, 5 grams protein, 147 milligrams sodium, 1 gram dietary fiber.

Small, Tart, Convenient

By definition, convenience foods are easy to prepare and serve.

The problem with many of them is they are loaded with salt, sugar, high-fructose corn syrup, trans fats and a host of other ingredients that may speed things along but aren't necessarily good for you.

The Star's recipe for Lemon Tartlets with Blueberries incorporates two high-quality convenience foods: sweetened condensed milk and graham cracker crumbs.

Sweetened condensed milk is a velvety, cream-colored mixture that has had about 60 percent of the water evaporated from it. Sugar is added to retard bacterial growth. More recently, low-fat and fat-free versions of condensed milk became available. Although the low-fat version has no fewer calories than the regular version, it does cut the fat in half.

Long before refrigeration and sophisticated preservation techniques were widespread, shelf-stable canned milk was frequently used in place of fresh milk, which was often teeming with bacteria that made people "milksick."

Gail Borden came up with the idea for portable canned milk while on a trans-Atlantic trip in 1852. By 1856 he had invented and patented condensed milk. He is credited with keeping soldiers fed during the Civil War and improving infant and child nutrition.

Graham crackers were invented in the 1830s by the Rev. Sylvester Graham, a dietary reformer who touted the whole-wheat cracker sweetened with honey as a health food, according to *The New Food Lover's Companion* by Sharon Tyler Herbst.

Finally, the blueberries add important antioxidants while individual tartlets help with portion control. The delightful pucker power of the lemon flavoring may mean you're satisfied with just half a tartlet instead of a whole one.

Lemon Tartlets
With Blueberries

Makes 6 tartlets

1 1/2 cups graham cracker crumbs
3 tablespoons sugar
3 tablespoons butter, melted
1 teaspoon vanilla extract
1 egg white, lightly beaten
3 eggs
1 (14-ounce) can low-fat sweetened condensed milk
1/2 cup freshly squeezed lemon juice
1 tablespoon grated lemon zest
1 cup fresh blueberries, rinsed

Preheat oven to 350 degrees. Coat six (4 1/2-inch) individual tartlet pans with removable bottoms with nonstick vegetable cooking spray.

In a mixing bowl, combine graham cracker crumbs and sugar. Stir in butter, vanilla and egg white, mixing well. Divide mixture evenly between tartlet pans. Press mixture into bottom and sides of pans. Place pans on a baking sheet. Bake 13 to 15 minutes. Let cool completely on wire rack.

Reduce oven temperature to 325 degrees. Whisk eggs in a mixing bowl. Add sweetened condensed milk and combine slightly. And lemon juice and lemon zest and combine well. Pour about 1/3 cup into each tartlet pan. Bake 20 to 25 minutes or until filling is set; don't over bake. Let tarts cool completely. Add fresh blueberries as a topping.

Per tartlet: 433 calories (32 percent from fat), 16 grams total fat (8 grams saturated), 131 milligrams cholesterol, 64 grams carbohydrates, 10 grams protein, 308 milligrams sodium, 1 gram dietary fiber.

Shopping Tips: Be sure to use fresh lemons; they have a less tinny flavor than pre-squeezed juice.

A Berry Colorful, Festive Treat

Photo by Jill Toyoshiba • THE KANSAS CITY STAR

In today's typical supermarket dairy case, yogurt is ubiquitous.

Just one company produces 6 million cups of yogurt a day in almost 100 flavors, styles and sizes, including spoon-less versions such as grab-and-go tubes and drinkable, energy-boosting formulations. But yogurt's popularity and health-conscious aura is relatively recent.

The nomadic tribes of Turkey discovered the joys of tart, fermented milk, and many ancient cultures throughout the Balkans, the Middle East and India have incorporated yogurt in their culinary traditions. Because of its naturally tart flavor, yogurt was a harder sell in the United States.

Although Turkish and Armenian immigrants are credited with bringing yogurt to these shores in the early 1900s, it wasn't until Danone (Americanized to Dannon) began to market fruit-sweetened yogurt in earnest in the 1970s that Americans began to develop a taste for it.

The Star's Red, White And Blue Yogurt Parfaits combine nonfat flavored yogurt with layers of nutrient-rich blueberries and strawberries. The use of fresh frozen blueberries whirled in a food processor lends the yogurt a mousse-like consistency that is "perfect" (and, coincidentally, the French translation for parfait).

Yogurt has been thought to promote good health since ancient times, and plenty of recent science supports that belief.

Yogurt with live active cultures is credited with helping to improve immune function by promoting the "good" bacteria in the digestive tract. It also contains protein, calcium, phosphorous, potassium and B vitamins, and it's easier to digest than milk, which is why it's considered a universal food good for everyone from toddlers to seniors.

Red, White And Blue Yogurt Parfait

Makes 4 servings

1 cup nonfat blueberry yogurt
1 cup fresh blueberries, frozen
   (do not thaw to prepare this recipe)
1 cup nonfat vanilla-flavored yogurt
1 cup sliced strawberries and blueberries
Mint for garnish

Place blueberry yogurt and frozen blueberries in food processor. Process quickly until smooth. Divide blueberry mixture into 4 small parfait or dessert glasses. Spoon 1/4 cup vanilla yogurt over blueberry mixture in each parfait glass. Layer strawberries over vanilla yogurt. Garnish with mint. Serve immediately.

Per serving: 134 calories (3 percent from fat), trace total fat (trace saturated fat), 2 milligrams cholesterol, 28 grams carbohydrates, 6 grams protein, 80 milligrams sodium, 2 grams dietary fiber.

Pump It Up: To get the most from your yogurt, choose brands that include live, active cultures, including acidophilus and bifidum.

SERVING TIPS: You can make this parfait in custard cups, but a wine glass makes a fun, pretty presentation. For children, freeze blueberry yogurt mixture in paper cups with wooden sticks.

Photo by Tammy Ljungblad • THE KANSAS CITY STAR

A Wee Indulgence, Oui

Just three bites.

That's how to stay slim says Mireille Guiliano, author of the best-seller *French Women Don't Get Fat: The Secret of Eating for Pleasure* (Alfred Knopf).

A fan of small indulgences and the svelte CEO of the champagne house Veuve Clicquot, Guiliano insists the most intense satisfaction from food often comes in the first few bites.

Of course, the idea of noshing is cross cultural. For instance, Spaniards have tapas, their version of small plates. The Chinese make a ritual out of nibbling appetizer-size morsels from dim sum carts. The Japanese create lavish mini feasts in bento boxes.

The holiday season is the perfect time to put Guiliano's three-bite theory to the test with *The Star's* Mini Candied Cranberry Chocolate Cupcakes.

The recipe requires an investment in mini-muffin

STORAGE TIP: If you want a bite but you're not up for serving a crowd, freeze half of the cupcakes before adding the cranberry topping. The topping recipe can be halved easily.

pans, but in addition to keeping portions in check, the tiny cupcakes are just the right-size nibble for a holiday party.

The topping—candied cranberries and a seemingly decadent drizzle of vanilla-flavored almond bark—makes a particularly elegant presentation.

As a bonus, the cocoa and cranberries contain powerful antioxidants.

Mini Candied Cranberry Chocolate Cupcakes

Makes 18 servings

3/4 cup sugar
5 tablespoons butter, softened
1 teaspoon vanilla extract
2 eggs
1 cup all-purpose flour
1/4 cup unsweetened cocoa
1/2 teaspoon baking soda
1/4 teaspoon salt
1/2 cup fat-free skim milk
For candied cranberries:
1 (12-ounce) package fresh cranberries
2/3 cup sugar
2 ounces vanilla-flavored almond bark

Preheat oven to 350 degrees. Beat together sugar, butter and vanilla at medium speed on electric mixer until well blended, about 3 minutes.

Add eggs, one at a time, beating well after each addition. Combine flour, cocoa, baking soda and salt. Add flour mixture to sugar mixture alternately with milk, beginning and ending with flour and mixing well after each addition.

Line mini-muffin tins with paper liners. Fill muffin cups 2/3 full. Bake 10 to 12 minutes or until pick inserted in center is clean when removed. Cool on wire rack.

Meanwhile, line a 10-by-15-inch pan with aluminum foil. Toss cranberries with 2/3 cup sugar. Bake at 350 degrees 15 minutes, stirring every 5 minutes. Cool completely.

Arrange 3 or 4 cranberries in center of each mini cupcake. Melt almond bark in microwave oven according to package directions. Place melted almond bark in zip-top plastic food bag and snip corner. Drizzle over cupcakes.

Per serving: 144 calories (25 percent from fat), 4 grams total fat (2 grams saturated), 30 milligrams cholesterol, 25 grams carbohydrates, 2 grams protein, 108 milligrams sodium, 1 gram dietary fiber.

Shopping Tips: Look for almond bark in the baking aisle of most supermarkets.

Buy fresh cranberries when in season and freeze for use throughout the year.

Photo by Tammy Ljungblad • THE KANSAS CITY STAR

Tiny Tart Packs Powerful Pucker

From the doll-sized Japanese eggplant sold at the farmers market to the pre-portioned, 100-calorie snack packs sold in vending machines, small portions have become big news.

But when I Googled recipes for Key lime pie, a distinctive summertime dessert favorite, I found one wedge weighed in at no less than 540 calories and 22 grams of fat per serving.

Key Lime Tartlets, on the other hand, fit perfectly with a miniature mind-set. The Star's recipe offers a satisfying three- to four-bite treat made with fat-free condensed milk and fresh juice. Yet the tiny pie still manages to deliver big flavor—at just 151 calories and 3 grams of fat.

If a diminutive dessert sounds like a fussy undertaking, read on.

Instead of using a specialty tart pan purchased at a gourmet cooking store, these tartlets are made in a standard muffin tin lined with ordinary crinkle paper cups.

While many home cooks have come to rely on convenience products such as the graham cracker crumb crust, here's an even tastier shortcut: Place a store-bought gingersnap cookie in the bottom of the muffin tin's cupcake liner. When the custard is baked, the gingersnap softens to form a ready-made crust without any muss or fuss.

Finally, the intensity of lime flavor comes from the use of fresh juice instead of bottled. But if you can't find Key limes, don't sweat it. Key limes are smaller— but not necessarily tarter—than standard Persian limes stocked yearround at supermarkets. Feel free to substitute.

Key lime was once considered an exclusively regional flavor, but now you can find Key lime ice cream, yogurt and even power bars at the corner convenience store.

Key Lime Tartlets

Makes 12 servings

12 crisp gingersnap cookies
3 eggs, at room temperature
1 (14-ounce) can fat-free sweetened
    condensed milk
3/4 cup freshly squeezed lime juice
    plus grated lime zest from all limes
    (about 6 to 7 Persian limes
    or 12 to 14 Key limes)
1/3 cup heavy whipping cream, whipped
1 teaspoon vanilla extract

Shopping Tip: Looking for an easy way to zest a lime? Try a Microplane Zester, available at microplane.com.

Preheat oven to 325 degrees. Line 12 muffin cups with paper liners. Spray each paper liner with nonstick vegetable cooking spray. Place a cookie in each paper liner.

Whisk together eggs, milk, lime juice, lime zest and vanilla until well blended. Pour a scant 1/4 cup lime mixture into each cup. Bake 16 to 19 minutes or until firm; do not overbake. Allow hot tarts to set in pan about 10 minutes. Carefully lift each tart from the pan and place on a tray. Cool completely, then refrigerate several hours or overnight. Dollop with 1 tablespoon whipped cream flavored with vanilla.

Per serving: 151 calories (19 percent from fat), 3 grams total fat (2 grams saturated), 9 milligrams cholesterol, 28 grams carbohydrates, 3 grams protein, 82 milligrams sodium, trace dietary fiber.

COOKING TIPS: Limes are easier to juice if left out at room temperature, then rolled on a countertop to release the juice before squeezing.

SERVING TIPS: You may substitute frozen, nondairy whipped topping (light or fat free), thawed, for whipped cream. Use Key lime slices, or zest, to garnish.

Bite-Size Cakes Satisfy Craving

Photo by Tammy Ljungblad • THE KANSAS CITY STAR

Even a chunky cherub knows angel food cake can help lighten the pudge.

The puffy, cloudlike confection is low in calories and fat and contains absolutely no cholesterol. A prudent dessert choice for anyone watching their waistline, the only downside is the cake requires separating and whipping egg whites until they form peaks.

True, the whipping can be a bit of a chore, but the flavor difference is far superior to a boxed mix. And since you're using a mixer to beat the whites, it's not likely you'll break a sweat.

Perfect for a brunch or shower, *The Star's* Lemon Angel Bites are small but still glamorous, especially when drizzled with a bright lemony glaze. A typical slice of angel food cake from a mix contains about 128 calories, according to the USDA's Nutrient Data Laboratory (nal.usda.gov/fnic/food comp/search). At just 41 calories per "bite," a serving of three cakes can satisfy a craving for something sweet.

Now who's feeling downright devilish?

SHOPPING TIPS: Cake flour is fine-textured soft wheat flour with a high starch content that makes light, white and tender baked goods. Usually packaged in 2-pound boxes, look for Softasilk or Swans Down brands in the baking aisle. Do not substitute all-purpose flour.

Superfine sugar is available in the baking aisle of most supermarkets. It dissolves quickly, a trait that makes it perfect for meringues. If you don't have superfine sugar, you can grind granulated sugar in a food processor.

Lemon Angel Bites

Makes 40 mini angel bites

1 cup superfine sugar, divided
1/2 cup plus 3 tablespoons cake flour
3/4 cup egg whites (5 to 6 eggs)
1/2 teaspoon salt
3/4 teaspoon cream of tartar
1/2 teaspoon vanilla extract
1 teaspoon grated lemon zest
2 tablespoons freshly squeezed lemon juice
3/4 cup confectioners' sugar
Additional grated lemon zest for garnish, if desired

Preheat oven to 375 degrees. Sift 1/4 cup sugar and flour together two times; set aside.

Place egg whites, salt and cream of tartar in mixing bowl. Beat with mixer on high speed until egg whites form medium peaks. Sprinkle remaining 3/4 cup sugar over egg whites and beat until thick and shiny. Add vanilla and zest and beat just until blended.

Sprinkle flour mixture over egg whites in 3 batches and fold in gently with rubber spatula. Spoon batter into ungreased mini muffin tins. Fill the cups almost full. Bake 12 to 15 minutes or until cakes are golden brown.
Allow to cool in the muffin pans, then gently use a butter knife to remove to a wire rack placed over a cookie sheet.

Whisk together lemon juice and confectioners' sugar until blended. Lightly dip tops of angel cakes in glaze then place on wire rack, glaze side up. Sprinkle lightly with additional lemon zest, if desired.

Per bite: 41 calories (none from fat), trace fat (no saturated fat), no cholesterol, 9 grams carbohydrates, 1 gram protein, 34 milligrams sodium, no dietary fiber.

Equipment Tips: For portion control, you will need mini muffin pans. To add air, you'll also need a sifter. Both items are widely available in supermarkets.

Berries Burst With Benefits

Photo by David Eulitt • THE KANSAS CITY STAR

Like seeds and nuts, berries have been a staple food from the beginning.

"We have been eating berries since we've been walking the Earth," says Steven Pratt, author of *SuperFoods HealthStyle* (William Morrow). "We ate them fresh in the summer. And dried, they kept all winter."

North American Indians ate pemmican, a mixture of meat or fish, hot fat and crushed berries. In addition to being nutritious, the berries helped preserve the meat.

More recently, the blueberry—a cultivated plant that thrives in the northern United States—has received the lion's share of positive press. But strawberries, raspberries and blackberries have similar nutrition profiles, each rich in antioxidants, compounds that may fight disease such as cancer and heart disease.

So did we really need modern science to confirm the benefits of a food humans have eaten for thousands of years?

"You know, there's no bad berry on the planet," Pratt says.

Ah, but what about when berries meet their one true match: cream.

Decadent?

Not if you're talking about an updated classic like *The Star's* Summer Berries With Yogurt Cream. Long considered a health food, most yogurt includes live active cultures that can keep the "good" bacteria in your body in check while providing protein, calcium and B vitamins.

To be sure the yogurt contains live cultures, Pratt advises consumers to look for L. acidophilus and S. thermophilus on the label. Some yogurts also contain L. bulgaricus, B. bifidus, L. casei and L. reuteri. Seek out yogurts that contain a variety of cultures, because each has health benefits.

Summer Berries With Yogurt Cream

Makes 4 servings

1 pint strawberries, hulled and cut in half
2 cups mixed berries such as blueberries,
   raspberries or blackberries
1 tablespoon orange juice
1 tablespoon sugar
1 teaspoon balsamic vinegar
2 tablespoons heavy cream
1/2 cup nonfat vanilla yogurt
1/2 teaspoon vanilla extract

Preparation Tip: Never wash berries until you are ready to use them.

Toss fruit with juice, sugar and vinegar. Allow to stand for 15 minutes. Toss again.

Whisk cream until slightly thickened. Fold into yogurt with vanilla. Serve berries in stemmed glasses and dollop with yogurt.

Per serving: 130 calories (22 percent from fat), 3 grams total fat (2 grams saturated), 11 milligrams cholesterol, 24 grams carbohydrates, 3 grams protein, 27 milligrams sodium, 4 grams dietary fiber.

COOKING TIP: When you toss fruit with juice and vinegar and let it sit, you're macerating, a fancy-schmancy culinary term that means soaking fruit in a liquid to absorb flavor. The Italians have long known that strawberries have an affinity for cream flavored with balsamic vinegar.

SHOPPING TIPS: Ripe strawberries are brightly colored and should have their green tops attached; smaller strawberries also tend to have a deeper flavor.

When choosing blueberries, look for a silvery "frost" on the skin and avoid any that are shriveled or mushy.

Raspberries should be firm and plump and missing their hulls; if the hull is attached the berries are immature and will be quite tart. Also look for blackberries that are dark, plump and missing their hulls.

Berry Torte Is A Patriotic Treat

God bless Mother Nature for juicy summer berries that ripen just in time for the Fourth of July. Dreaming up red, white and blue food can be a stretch, even if food marketers have made it their business to dream up all manner of unnatural color combinations.

Red, white and blue frosted Pop Tarts, anyone?

If you're looking for an edible triumvirate that is as delicious as it is patriotic, try *The Star's* Patriotic Fruit Torte, which resembles the American flag, thanks to a strawberry filling, a helping of blueberries and a fluffy angel food cake.

At our house, dessert is an all-American tradition. A right, even for those concerned with good nutrition. Now, I try to tell the kids that fruit is a dessert. But most of the time, they don't buy it. Still they can't seem to resist mixed berries spooned over angel food cake.

Strawberries contain plenty of anthocyanins, natural plant pigments that function as an antioxidant, and ellagic acid that is believed to help neutralize carcinogenic agents. They also contain plenty of vitamin C.

Made with beaten egg whites, angel food cake contains no fat or cholesterol. The only problem is making the cake from scratch involves separating a lot of eggs—not my favorite chore.

Always skeptical of shortcuts that churn out poor results, I tested this recipe with a boxed cake mix. (If you can find the right shape, you could even buy a cake and just assemble.) I taste-tested the boxed cake, which is a cinch to make, on the kids. My 11-year-old son and 6-year-old daughter thought it tasted great. Almost homemade, even.

Once I had unmolded the cake from its loaf pan, I was wowed by the visual presentation. And, yes, I had to admit that once topped with juicy berries, a dollop of yogurt (for calcium!) and toasted nuts (good fat!), it was a great holiday dessert with a minimal amount of assembly required.

Lunchbox Peanut Butter Cookies

Makes 16 cookies

1 cup plus 2 tablespoons all-purpose flour
1/2 teaspoon baking soda
1/2 teaspoon salt
1/4 cup butter
1/4 cup reduced-fat creamy peanut butter
1/4 cup plus 2 tablespoons
   packed dark brown sugar
1 egg
1 teaspoon vanilla extract
16 mini chocolate kisses

Shopping Tip: This recipe was tested with Hershey Mini Kisses.

Preheat oven to 350 degrees. Spray baking sheet with nonstick vegetable cooking spray.

Combine flour, baking soda and salt; set aside. In mixer bowl, blend together butter and peanut butter. Add brown sugar, egg and vanilla; beating until fluffy. Gradually add flour mixture and beat until blended.

Drop 12 generous teaspoonfuls onto prepared baking sheet, forming 12 cookies. Lightly pat down to flatten, and place one mini kiss in the center of each cookie. Bake until browned on the bottom, 12 to 14 minutes.

Transfer cookies to wire rack. Repeat with remaining dough. Allow cookies to cool completely (at least 1 to 2 hours) before serving.

Per cookie: 105 calories (34 percent from fat), 4 grams total fat (2 grams saturated), 18 milligrams cholesterol, 15 grams carbohydrates, 3 grams protein, 178 milligrams sodium, 1 gram dietary fiber.

STORAGE TIP: Store in an airtight container for up to 1 week.

Pump Up The Benefits

Looking for a colossal dose of carotenoids? Call on the great pumpkin.

After the obligatory wedge of pumpkin pie for Thanksgiving dinner, this New World native always seems to get the boot. But before you push that can of pumpkin puree to the back of the pantry for another year, consider its health benefits.

For starters, 1/2 cup of canned pumpkin puree has 42 calories and 3.4 grams of fiber. Pumpkin is also a good source of potassium, iron, riboflavin, folic acid and vitamin C. But what has really grabbed nutrition headlines in recent years are two carotenoids known as alpha-carotene and beta-carotene, both powerful phytonutrients.

Like the deep orange, yellow or red fat-soluble compounds found in an array of fruits and vegetables, the winter gourd's bright orange flesh is nature's shorthand for carotenoids. The body turns the carotenoids into vitamin A, which helps boost the immune system and may reduce the risk of some cancers, cardiovascular disease, inflammatory conditions and macular degeneration.

The 2005 USDA Dietary Guidelines include a reference list of foods high in vitamin A, and pumpkin ranked fourth out of 21 common foods. Still, studies show most American adults don't get enough vitamin A in their diets.

Pumpkin can be cooked like any winter squash, then added to soups and stews. But to create another layer of flavor, simply add the puree to a traditional dessert. The Star's Pumpkin Gingerbread Bars are moist and cakey, flavored with the traditional molasses and powdered ginger.

Gingerbread is a good holiday choice because it is naturally low in fat and cholesterol. This recipe also is designed to keep the portion sizes in check.

Pumpkin Gingerbread Bars

Makes 12 servings

2 eggs
1/2 cup brown sugar
3/4 cup solid pack pumpkin
2 tablespoons molasses
1 teaspoon vanilla extract
3/4 cup all-purpose flour
1 teaspoon baking powder
1 teaspoon ground cinnamon
1 teaspoon ground ginger
1 tablespoon confectioners' sugar

Preheat oven to 375 degrees. Spray a 9-inch square pan with nonstick vegetable cooking spray.

Beat eggs with electric mixer at high speed 2 minutes. Add brown sugar 1 tablespoon at a time, beating well after each addition.

Add pumpkin, molasses and vanilla. Beat at medium speed 2 minutes.

Combine flour, baking powder, cinnamon and ginger; stir to blend. Add to pumpkin mixture; stir well.

Pour into prepared pan. Bake 20 minutes or until a wooden pick inserted in center comes out clean.

Let cool 10 minutes in pan; invert onto platter. Sprinkle with confectioners' sugar. Serve warm.

Per serving: 81 calories (10 percent from fat), 1 gram total fat (trace saturated), 31 milligrams cholesterol, 17 grams carbohydrates, 2 grams protein, 55 milligrams sodium, 1 gram dietary fiber.

Shopping Tip: Canned pumpkin is available year-round. A secret: Most professional chefs prefer the convenience and flavor of canned pumpkin over making their own puree. Just make sure you choose a can of pumpkin puree, not pumpkin pie filling that already contains spices.

Cobble Together Healthy Cobbler

Photo by David Eulitt • THE KANSAS CITY STAR

Nickelodeon's Dora the Explorer (a fan of blueberries) and SpongeBob Squarepants (who lives in a pineapple under the sea) are part of the latest marketing effort to get kids to eat more fruits and vegetables.

The popular cartoon characters are scheduled to appear on packets of apples slices and edamame. But such licensing deals only serve to point up why childhood obesity and poor nutrition are on the national stage.

Fewer than 15 percent of American children eat the recommended amount of fruits and vegetables each day. According to the USDA, 33 percent of a child's diet should be made up of fruits and vegetables yet half of all elementary school children eat no fruit and three in 10 children eat no more than a single serving of vegetables each day.

Fruit and vegetables provide important nutrients and minerals for proper growth and development. But many kids and parents remain confused by what constituted a serving so nutrition experts opted for "cups" instead.

Kidshealth.org breaks down the new recommendations by a child's age and gender:
• 4 to 8 year olds need 1 1/2 cups vegetables and 1 1/2 cups fruit
• 9 to 13 year old girls need 2 cups of vegetables and 1 1/2 cups fruit
• 9 to 13 year old boys need 2 1/2 cups vegetables and 1 1/2 cups fruit

Since children seldom eat fruit for dessert, The Star's Blueberry Peach Cobbler is a great way to add more fruit to your child's diet. Although cobblers are typically made in the summers when fresh fruit is most abundant, this cobbler can be made year-round using canned peaches and frozen blueberries.

Encouraging kids to cook can help them become more interested and aware of how good nutrition affects their health.

Blueberry Peach Cobbler

Makes 6 to 8 servings

1/4 cup butter, melted
2 (15-ounce) cans sliced peaches
    in light syrup, undrained
3/4 cup all-purpose flour
2/3 cup sugar
1 teaspoon baking powder
1/4 cup fat-free skim milk
2/3 cup fresh or frozen blueberries,
    well drained

Pump It Up: This cobbler is sweet enough you can skip the ice cream on top and the kids will never know.

Preheat oven to 375 degrees. Coat a 9-inch-square baking dish with nonstick vegetable cooking spray; add melted butter and set aside. Drain peaches, reserving 1/2 cup syrup, and set aside.

Combine flour, sugar and baking powder in a medium bowl. Add reserved peach syrup and milk to flour mixture, stirring just until moistened. Pour batter in prepared dish and top with peaches and blueberries. Do not stir. Bake 35 minutes or until golden.

Per serving, based on 6: 300 calories (23 percent from fat), 8 grams total fat (5 grams saturated), 21 milligrams cholesterol, 57 grams carbohydrates, 3 grams protein, 173 milligrams sodium, 4 grams dietary fiber.

Go Bananas For Dessert

Photo by Tammy Ljungblad • THE KANSAS CITY STAR

Slipping on a banana peel? The stuff of comedians. Slipping up on your diet? Not likely to elicit a belly laugh.

But for every decadent dessert, there is a lighter, leaner version.

A pared-down banana split, The Star's Glazed Bananas With Frozen Yogurt offers plenty of natural sweetness and creamy goodness without all the wretched excess.

"For the past 100 years, the concoction we call the Banana Split has been, if not America's most popular dessert, then surely the most visible culinary symbol of our national indulgence," Michael Turback writes in The Banana Split Book (Camino Books).

Indeed, a traditional banana split—with three scoops of ice cream, flavored syrups, whipped cream, nuts and a cherry on top—can blow a week's worth of otherwise conscientious eating by as much as 1,200 calories.

Dairy products add B vitamins, calcium and protein to the diet, and compared to ice cream, frozen yogurt typically contains less fat.

But the key to making this dessert really work for you is to keep the portion sizes realistic. Softball-size scoops at the local ice cream parlor may seem the norm, but a single serving of ice cream or frozen yogurt is actually just 1/2 cup—figure roughly the size of a tennis ball.

Whenever possible, nutrition experts encourage adding fruit to desserts, since Americans rarely get enough in their daily diet. Bananas have long been America's favorite fruit, and a small to medium banana is only 100 calories, no fat and only 1 milligram of sodium.

Bananas also add vitamins B6 and C, fiber and potassium to the diet. An important nutrient that helps to counteract the excess sodium in the typical American diet, the potassium in bananas can help control blood pressure.

Glazed Bananas With Frozen Yogurt

Makes 6 servings

2 tablespoons butter
1/4 cup dark brown sugar
1/4 teaspoon cinnamon
1/4 cup orange juice
3 bananas
3 cups frozen fat-free vanilla yogurt

Heat butter in a small skillet until melted. Add brown sugar, cinnamon and orange juice and cook, stirring frequently, until simmering. Cut bananas in half lengthwise and cut each half into 1-inch pieces. Add bananas to juice mixture, cooking 3 to 5 minutes, turning as needed to coat with mixture. Serve over frozen yogurt.

Per serving: 218 calories (16 percent from fat), 4 grams total fat (2 grams saturated), 10 milligrams cholesterol, 44 grams carbohydrates, 5 grams protein, 108 milligrams sodium, 1 gram dietary fiber.

COOKING TIPS: Wash bananas before peeling since bacteria on the peel can be transferred to the fruit.

For easier scooping, be sure to set the frozen yogurt out 10 to 15 minutes before serving to allow it to soften.

Shopping Tips: When choosing a brand of frozen yogurt, be sure to read the nutrition label. Frozen yogurt comes in a dizzying array of flavors, as well as widely varying fat and calorie counts. If possible, choose a fat-free version. To analyze this recipe we used a fat-free brand that contains 90 calories per serving.

Photo by Tammy Ljungblad • THE KANSAS CITY STAR

A Berry Good Sorbet

Skip the milk and cream. For a truly light and refreshing summer dessert, scoop up some sorbet.

Although you can certainly find plenty of luscious flavors and a variety of brands in your grocer's freezer case, sorbet is a cinch to make at home. Unlike ice cream, no special equipment is required.

A great way to use some of the delicious, ripe berries available at the farmers market this time of year, sorbets are naturally rich in vitamins and minerals and contain little fat or cholesterol.

The Star's Raspberry Sorbet With Fresh Blackberries is an antioxidant-rich recipe loaded with folate, fiber and phytonutrients that may help improve memory and reduce the risk for developing heart disease and cancer.

Top with a sprig of mint and you have a restaurant-quality dessert or palate cleanser.

SERVING TIP: For a truly dramatic presentation, use clear glass compote dishes or wine glasses to show off the sorbet's beautiful, rich magenta color.

Raspberry Sorbet With Fresh Blackberries

Makes 6 servings

1 cup sugar
1 cup water
6 to 8 fresh mint leaves
3 cups fresh raspberries
1/2 cup orange juice
1 1/2 cups fresh blackberries
2 tablespoons orange-flavored liqueur
Fresh mint leaves for garnish, optional

Combine sugar, water and mint leaves in a saucepan. Heat to a boil; reduce heat and cook, stirring frequently, 3 to 4 minutes or until sugar is dissolved. Remove from heat and allow to cool.

Place raspberries and orange juice in work bowl of food processor. Process until smooth. Combine raspberry puree and sugar-water mixture; pour through a sieve to remove seeds and mint leaves. Pour into a freezer container, cover and freeze several hours or overnight. Stir mixture 2 or 3 times in the first 2 hours.

When ready to serve, allow mixture to stand at room temperature 10 to 15 minutes to thaw slightly. Combine blackberries and orange liqueur and allow to stand 10 to 15 minutes.

Using an ice cream scoop, scoop frozen mixture into balls and place in individual dessert dishes. Top each with about 1/4 cup fresh blackberries. Garnish with mint leaves.

Per serving: 204 calories (2 percent from fat), 1 gram total fat (no saturated fat), no cholesterol, 48 grams carbohydrates, 1 gram protein, 1 milligram sodium, 7 grams dietary fiber.

KITCHEN EQUIPMENT TIPS: If you don't own a conical metal sieve with a wooden pestle (available at housewares stores), you may want to consider buying one. It's a small investment with a big return.

A tip from *Brilliant Food Tips and Cooking Tips* (Rodale) by David Joachim: To clean a clogged sieve, soak in hot, soapy water then scrub with a vegetable brush.

Shopping Tip: If you don't keep a bottle of Grand Marnier in the pantry, you can save money by buying a mini bottle of the liqueur instead.

Watermelon Is 'Lycopene Leader'

Photo by David Eulitt • THE KANSAS CITY STAR

Watermelon has always been an icon of summer. Served at picnics, backyard barbecues and patio parties, the seed-speckled red flesh is synonymous with thirst-quenching relief from the scorching heat.

Although cut-up cubes have become a year-round staple of supermarket salad bars, the fruit is at its peak from mid-June to late August.

While watermelon is rarely thought of as a nutritional powerhouse, the National Watermelon Promotion Board (watermelon.org) has begun to describe its star client as so packed with the good stuff that it is "practically a multivitamin unto itself." Fat-free and low in calories, watermelon is a fair to good source of vitamins A, B6 and C; thiamine; and potassium, a mineral essential to water balance in the body.

The watermelon marketing gurus have also been quick to tout their boy as the "lycopene leader" after studies revealed it contains plenty of lycopene, a carotenoid pigment that gives watermelon its red hue. Lycopene has been linked to reduced risk of heart attack and certain cancers.

The watermelon board also has funded some studies by the USDA's Agricultural Research Service (ars.usda.gov/is/AR/archive/jun02/lyco0602.htm) looking into watermelon's levels of lycopene: 1 1/2 cups of ripe, red watermelon contains 9 to 13 milligrams of lycopene. That's about 40 percent more than raw tomatoes, which were previously thought to be the leading fruit or vegetable source.

Now agricultural researchers are studying just how available lycopene in watermelon is to the body and how growing conditions and seed varieties may affect the final nutrient content.

The Star's Frozen Watermelon Lemonade combines the flavors of watermelon, lemon, raspberry and strawberry to create an outrageously delicious way to tame the summer rays. The "lemonade" can be served as a slushy or a more elegant sorbet.

Frozen Watermelon Lemonade

Makes 6 to 8 servings

3 cups watermelon cubes, seeds removed
1/2 cup raspberries
3/4 cup sugar
1/2 cup water
Juice of 2 lemons (about 1/2 cup)
1 1/2 cups strawberry-flavored, calorie-free
     carbonated water, chilled

Place watermelon cubes and raspberries in blender; process until smooth. Pour juice through a sieve; discard pulp.

Combine sugar and water in a small saucepan. Heat, stirring constantly, just until sugar dissolves. Set aside and allow to cool slightly.

Stir sugar-water and lemon juice into watermelon raspberry juice mixture. Pour juice mixture into a covered freezer container. Freeze until firm.

Using an ice cream scoop, spoon mixture into tall glasses. Pour 3 to 4 tablespoons strawberry-flavored water over frozen juice in each glass. Serve immediately.

Per serving, based on 6: 131 calories (2 percent from fat), trace total fat (no saturated fat), no cholesterol, 33 grams carbohydrates, 1 gram protein, 3 milligrams sodium, 1 gram dietary fiber.

SHOPPING TIP: It's true: The best way to tell whether a watermelon is ripe is to thump it. (It should sound hollow.) But if you don't want to wrestle with a watermelon the size of the Goodyear blimp, look for a personal-size variety.

Whole melons better preserve the nutrient content, but if you refuse to mess with the seeds and sticky rind, head to the salad bar for precut watermelon cubes, even better if they're seedless.

Serving Tips: To serve as sorbet, freeze juice mixture in an 8-inch square dish. Omit strawberry-flavored carbonated water. Using a small scoop, shape frozen juice mixture into balls and arrange in individual serving dishes. Garnish, if desired, with a fresh mint sprig.

Index